The

DEAD SEA SCROLLS

AND

Primitive Christianity

JEAN DANIÉLOI

Professeur d'histoire des origines chrétiens
à l'Institut Catholique de Pa

AD SEA SCROLLS
AND

Primitive Christianity

HELICON PRESS, Inc., *Baltimore, Maryland* Translated from the French by SALVATOR ATTANASI

Library of Congress Catalog Card No 58-11448

First published in France by Editions de l'Orante under the title
Les Manuscrits de la Mer Morte et les origines du Christianisme

This edition first published 1958

© 1958 by Helicon Press Inc

NIHIL OBSTAT   Edward A Cerny, S S , D D
           Censor Librorum

IMPRIMATUR· ✠   Most Reverend Francis P Keough, D D
           Archbishop of Baltimore
                           September 11, 1958

The *Nihil Obstat* and *Imprimatur* are official declarations that a book or
pamphlet is free of doctrinal or moral error No implication is contained
therein that those who have granted the *Nihil Obstat* and *Imprimatur*
agree with the opinions expressed

Printed in the U.S.A by Garamond Press, Baltimore Md.

Helicon Press, 5305 East Drive, Baltimore 27, Md

Preface

It is in no wise the purpose of this book to provide a
history of the discovery of the Dead Sea Scrolls nor to
make an assessment of their contents. For this the
reader is referred to the works of eminent specialists in
this field such as Prof. Millar Burrows, Father R. de
Vaux, Prof. W. H Brownlee, Prof. Dupont-Sommer,
Father J. T. Milik and many others. The only question
we wish to examine here—or at least to pose correctly—
is that of the relations between the religious group
which we know through the Scrolls and the origins of
Christianity.

The immense interest aroused in this question and
the freakish considerations it has sometimes occasioned
in scholarly circles led me to make an attempt at
establishing a basic orientation towards the question of
the Scrolls in a series of lectures delivered last year.
This book contains the complete text of these three
lectures, to which have been added some further reference material and bibliographical footnotes. Refer-

5

ences to the New Testament are founded on numerous studies already published, and in this book I merely wish to point out the results of this research.

It should be clear that this study is but a bare outline. Before a deeper one can be made, it will be necessary for all the relevant documents to be published and all comparisons and collations to be finished. Nevertheless, it is possible to trace the broad outlines of such a study. It will be seen how such tracings renew our traditional picture of Christian origins and permit us to fill in the setting within which the life of Christ and the beginnings of the Church unfolded. Finally, such tracings will also make us better understand the originality and uniqueness of Christianity itself.

Contents

Abbreviations

I. QUMRAN SCROLLS

DSH	:	Commentary on the Book Of Habakkuk
DSD	:	The Manual of Discipline
DST	:	The Book of Hymns or Psalms of Thanksgiving
DSW	:	The War of the Sons of Light and the Sons of Darkness
CDC	:	The Zadokite Document (Damascus Document)
1 QSa	·	Manual of Discipline for the Future Congregation of Israel
1 QBen	:	Collection of Blessings from Cave 1
4 QT	.	Collection of *Testimonia* from Cave 4
4 QpGen	:	Commentary on the Genesis from Cave 4
4 QpIsa	:	First Commentary on the Isaias of Cave 4

II. PERIODICALS

BASOR	:	Bulletin of the American Schools of Oriental Research
ET	:	Evangelische Theologie
JBL	:	Journal of Biblical Literature
JJS	:	Journal of Jewish Studies
PEQ	:	Palestine Exploration Quarterly
RB	.	Revue Biblique
RHPR	:	Revue d'histoire et de philosophie religieuse
RHR	:	Revue de l'histoire des religions
SC	:	Studia Catholica
ST	:	Studia Theologica
TZ	:	Theologische Zeitschrift
VT	·	Vetus Testamentum
ZKT	:	Zeitschrift für Katholische Theologie
ZKT	:	Zeitschrift für Theologie und Kirche

I

The Religious Community
of Qumran and
the Evangelical Milieu

I T IS not my intention here to discuss what is contained in the scrolls discovered in the caves near
the Dead Sea. It will suffice to recall that in 1947 a
Bedouin accidentally stumbled upon the first cave
which contained the most valuable of the scrolls: the
*Commentary on the Book of Habakkuk; the Book of
Hymns or Psalms of Thanksgiving; the War of the Sons
of Light and the Sons of Darkness;* and the *Apocryphal
Genesis,* recently unrolled. Two other caves were
discovered in February-March 1952, one of which
contained two copper scrolls. I was at Qumran on
September 1 of that same year, and Father de Vaux
told me it looked as though there would be no further
discoveries. A fortnight later the Bedouins discovered
Cave 4, the richest of all. Finally, seven other caves
containing fragments of lesser importance were also
discovered.

At the same time, the excavations being carried out
at the foot of the rocky cliff lying between Qumran and
the Dead Sea led to the discovery of some ancient
archeological ruins, now almost entirely cleared away.
Coins found on this site, dating from 130 B.C. to

70 A.D., clearly established that this had been the monastery of the religious community to which the scrolls belonged. The geographical location, as well as the doctrines and ritual practices described in the texts, have permitted scholars, in particular Prof. Dupont-Sommer, to identify this community with the Essenes about whom we had already known from the writings of Josephus and Philo the Jew. In this connection I refer the reader to the book written by Millar Burrows.[1]

A discovery of this kind is in itself quite sensational. But what endows it with a unique significance and character is that it bears a direct relation to the problem of the origins of Christianity, which is one of the most intriguing and exciting problems of historical research. As a matter of geographical fact, the Essenian community did live in Palestine and, more specifically, in a region visited by Christ. Historically, the final phase of its history encompasses a period of time that coincides exactly with the life of Christ and the first developments of the Church. The first question, then, that immediately comes to mind is: Did early Christianity have any contacts with this community? A comparative study of the documents permits one to state that such contacts did indeed take place. In this book we shall deal with the following questions· What was the nature of these contacts? What do Christianity and Essenism

[1]*The Dead Sea Scrolls*, Viking Press, 1955. French readers are referred to Geza Vermès' book, *Les Manuscrits du désert de Juda*, Desclée et Cie, 1953. The *Revue Biblique*, particularly the articles by Father deVaux, is indispensable for keeping up with the actual progress of the discoveries.

have in common? Wherein lies the uniqueness and distinctiveness of Christianity?

First we shall assess the nature of the undeniable relations that existed between these two movements during the first period of Christianity—during its very birth. The central question of the relations between Christ and the Teacher of Righteousness will be reserved for the second chapter. And finally, in the third chapter, we shall deal with the first phases in the development of the Church.

John the Baptist and Qumran

The question of the contacts between John the Baptist and the hermits of the desert of Judah is not new. For a long time certain scholars have suggested that the Precursor be viewed as one of those who up to then were known only under the name of Essenes. But the discovery of the manuscripts has in an undeniable way confirmed the Baptist's contacts with the monks of Qumran, whom we know to be identical with the Essenes.[2] This is one of the first important results yielded by the research, and one of the first enigmas satisfactorily solved. Henceforth the mysterious figure of the Baptist stands out against a specific background

[2]See J. SCHMITT, "Les ecrits du Nouveau Testament et les texts de Qumran," *Rev SR*, XXIV, 1955, pp. 394-401; XXX, 1956, pp. 54-74.

instead of arising suddenly from an unknown world.[3]

Indeed, simple geographical data by themselves confirm the certainty of these contacts. The region in which John conducted his baptismal mission is that which surrounds the River Jordan just before it empties into the Dead Sea. Now the monastery of the Essenes was located about two miles south, on the western shore of the Dead Sea. Matthew calls this region "the desert of Judea," but Luke employs a different turn of phrase: "The word of the Lord was made unto John, the son of Zachary, in the desert" (*Luke* 3:2). It would seem that here the word "desert" designates a specific place, for this is the very word used by the hermits of Qumran to designate the region where they dwelt. Here then, "desert" does not designate just any wild or desolate spot but a precise location which, as Pliny the Elder has noted (*Hist. Nat.* V, 17), was planted with palm trees and watered by springs.

We have striking proof of the identity of the desert of Qumran and the desert of John the Baptist. It is known that the four Evangelists apply the words of Isaias to John: "The voice of one crying in the desert. Prepare ye the way of the Lord, make straight in the wilderness the paths of our God" (40:3). Now the Essenes had already been applying this text to themselves. It is mentioned twice in the *Manual of Discipline:* "When such things come to pass in the community of Israel, the men of Israel should remove

---

[3]This point has been the subject of an important study by Brownlee, "John the Baptist in the Light of the Ancient Scrolls," *Interpretation,* IX, 1955, pp. 78-86.

themselves from the society of wicked men in order to
go into the Desert and there prepare the way, as it is
written: 'Prepare ye the way of the Lord, make straight
in the wilderness the paths of our God'," (VIII, 12-14;
see also IX, 20). Such a similarity of content and
expression cannot be fortuitous. It leads us to assert a
similarity of views between John and the hermits of
Qumran as well as their identity in that both "prepare
the way for God."[*]

This leads us to investigate whether other points of
contact will emerge, and there are many as we shall see.
John came from a priestly family: his parents, Zachary
and Elizabeth, descended from Abia and Aaron (*Luke*
1:5). Now the people of Qumran also descended from
priestly families; hence the name by which they are
called in the scrolls, "the sons of Zadok." (Zadok was a
high priest during the reign of Solomon.) It is this
characteristic that makes them differ so fundamentally
from the Pharisees. It is therefore quite probable that
a contact was established between the family of John
and the men of Qumran. It will be noted that the
Benedictus, the hymn sung by Zachary at the birth of
his son, being in conformity with the Essenian custom
of composing hymns, also contains characteristic
expressions of the Qumran scrolls: "for thou shalt go . . .
to prepare his way," "to give knowledge of salvation,"
"the Orient from on high hath visited us" (an allusion
to the star of Jacob), and an imploration "to direct our
feet into the way of peace."

[*]Re the desert see also *Isaias* 2·7-11, and *Apoc.* 12·6, where the
idea of "preparation" is also to be found.

Having said this about the parents of John, we may ask the question: What about John himself? There is a passage in Luke which up to now has been entirely unintelligible, wherein we read that "... the child grew, and was strengthened in spirit; and was in the deserts until the day of his manifestation in Israel" (*Luke* 1:80). One finds it difficult to imagine a child growing up alone in the middle of a desert. But we have seen that the word "desert" refers to the monastery of the Essenes; and we also know, as Brownlee has noted, that the monks of Qumran boarded young boys. It is quite probable, therefore, that John's parents boarded their son with them just as the parents of Racine entrusted him to the hermits of Port-Royal.

The portrait that the Evangelists draw of the Precursor likewise offers details which coincide with what we now know about the people of Qumran. Thus his nourishment consisted of locusts and wild honey (*Matthew* 3:4). Now, the *Damascus Document* goes so far as to specify that locusts must be roasted. John abstained from wine and all fermented beverages, and certain evidence attests to the same practice among the Essenes (JEROME, *Adv. Jov.*, 2, 14).[5] In fact, John appears to have been an ascetic in every conceivable way, just as Christ himself will emphasize (*Luke* 7:13); and the ascetic character of the life of the monks of Qumran is one of the most distinctive features about

[5]See VERMES, *Les Manuscrits du désert de Juda*, pp. 60-61.

them. To this we add the fact that John was not married, and that celibacy was also one of the requirements of the sect of Qumran.

If we examine John's situation in relation to the different currents within the Judaism of the time, the first thing that strikes us is his contacts with the strange environment of the Herods. This, too, can straightway be explained on the basis of geographical propinquity. The Herods willingly resided in the locality of Qumran: they had a palace in Jericho, at present being excavated, and a fortress in Macheronte on the opposite shore of the Dead Sea, directly facing Qumran. John was in contact with Herod Antipas, one of the sons of Herod the Great, the Tetrarch of Galilee who appears in the Passion. Mark tells us that "Herod feared John, knowing him to be a just and holy man: and kept him, and when he heard him, did many things: and he heard him willingly" (6:20). It was with extreme reluctance that he sacrificed him to Herodias, and we read in Josephus that it was an Essene who predicted his future glory to Herod the Great (*Ant.*, XV, 10:5), and that another interpreted a dream for Archelaius, a brother of Herod Antipas (XVIII, 3:3).[6]

On the other hand, John reserves his severest criticism for the Pharisees and the Sadducees (*Matthew* 3:7), and this brings us face to face with one of the great enigmas to which the discoveries of

[6]On this point I disagree with C.-T. FRITSCH who is of the opinion that Herod the Great persecuted the Essenes, "Herod the Great and the Qumran Community," *JBL*, LXXIV, 1955, pp. 173-181.

Qumran have given rise. As a matter of fact Philo and Josephus always cite three great Jewish sects: the Pharisees, the Sadducees and the Essenes. The Essenes, however, are nowhere mentioned in the Gospels. Undoubtedly the solution to this puzzling question must be sought in the fact that John names only those sects to which he was opposed. If he makes no mention of the Essenes it is because he identifies himself with them, at least to a certain degree. And this is a new argument with which to establish the links that unite him with them.

But this is not yet the most startling aspect of the matter. That lies in the very teaching of the Baptist who announces that the Judgment of the world is imminent. This Judgment will be a divine action that will separate the wheat from the chaff (*Matthew* 3:12). It will comprise an effusion of the Holy Ghost and destruction by fire (*Matthew* 3:11). This Judgment will be carried out by one whose shoes John is not worthy of untying (*Matthew* 3:11). John's mission is to prepare hearts for this coming visit of God by preaching penance (*Matthew* 8:8). And the sign of this penance is the acceptance of baptism by water, which gains one entry to the eschatological community: belonging to the race of Abraham is not enough.

Now this can be found expressed in almost identical words in the Qumran scrolls. The principal text here is the *Commentary on the Book of Habakkuk*. In fact, the purpose of this commentary or *Midrash* is to show that the events predicted by Habakkuk as heralding the end of the world took place during the time of the establishment of the community, and that in particular they came to pass during the lifetime of the Teacher of Righteousness. And this indeed, as Karl Elliger[7] has observed, exhibits an astonishing resemblance to the manner in which the New Testament presents the prophecies as having been fulfilled by the events in the life of Christ. The most remarkable example is the one already cited of the prophecy of Isaias (40), a point to which we shall return later. Here we shall only make clear that for the people of Qumran, just as for John the Baptist, the end of days announced by the prophets has arrived.

Moreover, the events that constitute the end of days are described by John in terms closely resembling those used by the men of Qumran. A fundamental idea of the community, later to be found in the parables of Christ, is that the purpose of the Judgment is to separate the good from the wicked. This Judgment will consist of an effusion of the Holy Ghost: "Then God in His truth will cleanse all the works of each man, in order to purify them by the Spirit" (DSD, VI, 20). But it will also be a destruction of sinners by eternal fire (DSD, IV, 12-13), and this notion of destruction by fire is particularly important because it appears in the Qumran texts. One finds it again in the *Second Epistle of St. Peter* (2:12-13).

[7]*Studien zum Habakuk-Kommentar vom Toten Meer*, pp. 150-157.

The idea that one must prepare himself for the end of the world by doing penance is a familiar one in the Qumran scrolls. The sons of Zadok actually call themselves The Penitents. Further, they form a community of penitents; and the act of baptism constitutes entry to the community. And this is an extremely interesting point. One cannot help but be struck by the importance that ritual ablutions have for the sectarians of Qumran and for John, called the Baptist, and his followers. It is difficult not to think that there must have been a certain connection between the two practices.

It should be noted—and this notation will be of great importance for what is to follow—that if John the Baptist and the hermits of Qumran share the idea that the end of days has arrived with them, and that they are part of this event, they also agree in asserting that what has arrived with them is only the preparation for the last days, not the end of time itself. It should also be noted, as Brownlee has done, that when John is asked: "Art thou Elias? Art thou the prophet?" He answers: "No" (*John* 1:21). This was also the position of the Essenes. The Teacher of Righteousness, never represented himself as the Messiah, any more than did John the Baptist. This brings them together, but in a manner that reveals the radical contrast between them and Jesus on this question.

The fact remains that with respect to the eschatological climate of the time the resemblances between the group around Qumran and the group around the Baptist are striking. Must we conclude then that John is but a great Essenian prophet? It is possible that he may have been an Essene. But it is more probable that he was only deeply influenced by Essenism. What is certain, however, is that he had a personal vocation. "The word of the Lord was made unto John, the son of Zachary, in the desert" (*Luke* 3:2). He had therefore a distinctive message of his own and "John's disciples" on several occasions appear as a group quite distinct from Essenes (*John* 3:25). This indeed is manifested in certain characteristics peculiar to his mission. His preaching is addressed to all Jews (*Matthew* 3.5): John appears as someone sent by God to all Israel and even to publicans and sinners. Now this contrasts greatly with the closed character of the community of the pious priests of Qumran. The baptismal rite performed by John is also very different from the Essenian ablutions. The Essenian baptism was nothing more than admission to the daily baths of the community after a year-long novitiate. There are no indications that the first immersion had any special significance. The baptism performed by John, on the contrary, appears like a prophetic gesture, realizing the effusion of living waters announced by the prophets and preparing for the effusion of the Holy Ghost.

But this is not where the most important difference lies. The distinctive message of John is not, like that of the men of Qumran, only the announcing of the visitation of God, the coming of the Messiah, the effusion of the Spirit. His mission is to bear witness that the "visitation" has taken place, that the Messiah is already here, and that the Spirit is abroad. His mission is to designate Jesus as being the realization of the expected event. Indeed, his father Zachary did not speak of the "visitation" to come but he blessed the Lord "because he hath visited and wrought the redemption of his people" (*Luke* 1:58). John, himself, testifies to having seen the Spirit descend on Jesus and "gave testimony saying: . . . and I knew him not; but he who sent me to baptize with water, said to me: He upon who thou shalt see the Spirit descending, and remaining upon him, he it is that baptizeth with the Holy Ghost" (*John* 1:32-33). And this is why John designates him to his disciples saying, "Behold the Lamb of God."

Thus the community of Qumran allows us to re-discover the climate of Messianic expectation which was also shared by the group among whom John lived. It seems, moreover, that this eschatological expectation was more alive during the time of the Teacher of Righteousness than it was during the time of John the Baptist. It shows us how the coming of the Messiah appeared to be imminent, and therefore the men of Qumran mark a stage in the mystery of the Messianic waiting. But a final and decisive period opens with John, in which the Messiah is no longer expected but has already arrived. Thus John constitutes a link between the last moment of the Old Testament and the inauguration of the New. From now on his insertion in sacred history takes on its full significance; and the more apparent those traits which he had in common with the Essenes become the more so does his originality stand out.

Jesus and the Zadok Priests

Heretofore we have sought for the points of contact between the community of Qumran and the Johannine group. Now we come to the second issue, dealing with the contacts between the monks of Qumran and the Evangelists and their following. I clearly specify the point to which I shall confine myself in this chapter. In fact the question of the comparison between Christ and the Teacher of Righteousness is one of a different order. For the present we shall content ourselves with asking the question whether Christ had any contacts with the Essenian community of His time.

It appears evident that there were, if we recall the contacts that Christ had with John the Baptist at the time of His baptism. But one episode above all, that of the Temptation, here assumes its full significance. Matthew writes that Jesus was led by the Spirit to the desert to be tempted there (*Matthew* 4:1). Yet we have seen that the desert, otherwise not identified, would appear to designate the solitude of the Essenes, in view of the setting in which we find ourselves. Moreover, the traditional locus of the Temptation is on the very cliff, slightly north of Qumran, where the scrolls have been discovered. Thus the sojourn of Christ in the desert appears to be a retreat to a place of prayer. And it is the very theme of the Temptation that makes us think of the monks of Qumran: for them man was torn between the influence of demons and angels. This was the substance of their doctrine. Significantly, it is said that Christ was tempted by the devil and that later angels came to minister to Him (*Matthew* 4.11).

For that matter the very first acts of the public life of Christ, according to John, take place in the region around the mouth of the river Jordan. It is there that He recruits His first disciples, who seem to have belonged to the group around John the Baptist. They were waiting for the imminent coming of the Messiah. Later we shall have occasion to say that one of the disciples of Christ, namely St. John, holds to a view of things that seems to be deeply influenced by the conceptions prevalent in Qumran. Consequently one would be tempted to think that he was an Essene. In any case, as Cullman has shown, the disciples of the Baptist constitute an intermediate link between the men of Qumran and the disciples of Christ.[8] This is confirmed by the fact that the attitude of Jesus with regard to the Jewish sects is an extension of John's. The Essenes are never mentioned in the Gospels, and the reason for this may well be that for Christ they correspond to "the true Israelites," "the poor of Israel."

After making this assertion we can now point out more certain traces of contact between the milieu of Qumran and the milieu in which Christ recruited His first disciples. Initially it seems—and this is a very noteworthy point—that Jesus and His disciples followed the Qumran calendar. This important discovery was made by Mlle. Jaubert.[9] It is known that one of the

[8]"The Significance of the Qumran texts for research into the beginnings of Christianity," *JBL*, LXXIV, 1955, p. 219.
[9]"La date de la dernière Cène," *RHR*, 1954, pp. 140-176.

most difficult problems in the exegesis of the New Testament is that of establishing the exact day of the Last Supper. The synoptic Gospels make a paschal meal of it and fix the date as the evening of the 14th of Nisan, the first month of the Jewish ecclesiastical calendar, corresponding to March-April. But according to St. John the Crucifixion took place before Easter: Christ therefore was crucified on the day of the 14th of Nisan and He instituted the Eucharist on the 13th, in the evening. In this case the meal would no longer be a paschal banquet, which would contradict the synoptic Gospels, unless Christ advanced the date of the paschal meal. But what would be the explanation for this?

The problem would be solved if it could be shown that at that time there were two different dates for the celebration of Easter. Now there exists an old tradition according to which Christ is supposed to have partaken of the paschal meal on Tuesday evening, and to have been arrested on Wednesday and crucified on Friday. This tradition has been neglected up to now. Mlle. Jaubert has shown that the people of Qumran used an old ecclesiastical calendar of 364 days, containing four trimesters of 91 days, each of which had 13 weeks. Since there were exactly 52 weeks in the year, feast-days, according to this calendar, necessarily fell on the same day of the month *and of the week*. Furthermore, in this calendar Easter always fell on a Wednesday. The night before, therefore, was a Tuesday. Thus Christ must have celebrated the Last Supper on the eve of Easter according to the Essenian calendar. On the

other hand, He was supposed to have been crucified on
the eve of the official Easter which in that year fell on
Saturday.

Once the calendar of the Essenes disappeared, however, this date was erased from memory and the date
of the Last Supper was established either as Wednesday, according to John, or Thursday. The discovery of
the Qumran calendar permits the true date to be
restored and also provides an explanation for one of the
enigmas of the New Testament. Thus one can better
understand the significance of the events of the Passion, because heretofore it was difficult to see how the
multiple confrontations of Christ with Annas, with
Caiphas, and with Pilate could take place in a single
night. It is more satisfying to think that these encoun-
ters took up the days of Wednesday and Thursday.
And, in the last analysis a new relationship between
Christ and the milieu of Qumran has been established.

The question of the calendar is not only one which
suggests a relationship between the Last Supper and
the Qumran community. The very ceremony attending
the meal presents analogies. Matthew writes: "And
whilst they were at supper, Jesus took bread, and
blessed, and broke, and gave it to His disciples, and
said: Take ye, and eat. This is My body. And taking the
chalice, He gave thanks, and gave to them, saying:
Drink ye all of this. For this is My blood of the new
testament, which shall be shed for many unto remis-
sion of sins" (*Matthew* 26:26-28). Even though the
essential elements, namely the transformation by Christ

of the bread and wine, and the bond between the blood of Christ and the New Testament, have no counterpart in the Essenian texts, the very protocol of the meal recalls the meals of Qumran: "When they prepare the table to eat and wine to drink, the priest must be the first to extend his hand to bless the first portions of the bread. And if wine is being drunk, the priest must be the first to extend his hand to bless the first portion of the bread and the wine" (DSD, VI, 3-6). Such practices, however, were common to both the Essenes and other Jewish sects. Hence it cannot be said with certainty that Jesus had borrowed them from Qumran.

There is something that is even more strange, however. There is a fragment which describes the Messianic banquet: "When they gather around the table to eat or to drink wine, and the common board has been spread and the wine mixed, no one is to stretch out his hand for the first portion of bread or wine before the priest. For it is he who is to bless the first portion of bread and wine and the first to stretch out his hand to the bread. After that the Messiah of Israel will place his hands on the bread" (I QSa., II, 17-20, p. 117).

The words of Christ will be recalled: "But yet behold, the hand of him that betrayeth me is with me on the table" (*Luke* 22:21). Here above all it would seem that Christ's gesture makes manifest that He is the Messiah and the expected Priest.

As a result, the religious community established by Christ and His disciples has been viewed as presenting analogies with the community of Qumran. And this impression is reinforced by other characteristics. On the one hand Christ established a group of Twelve Apostles as the supreme council of the community founded by Him. This is evidently an allusion to the Twelve Sons of Jacob the chiefs of ancient Israel; and thereby Christ gives a sign that He is establishing a new Israel. But perhaps this can be seen in a more immediate context As a matter of fact it is worthy of note that at the head of the community of Qumran there was a council of twelve members and three priests. It is difficult to say whether the three priests were higher in authority than the twelve; but if such was the case, the resemblance would be even more striking because among the Twelve Apostles there was a privileged group of three—Peter, James and John.[10]

To this must be added the fact that the manner in which the Council of the Community is described singularly recalls what the New Testament says of the Twelve. In the *Manual of Discipline* we read: "The Council of the Community will be established like an evergreen plant, a sanctuary for Israel . . . its members witnesses to the truth in view of the coming Judgment . . . It will be a tested bulwark and a precious cornerstone; and its foundations will never shake nor be shaken" (DSD, VIII, 5-8).

Now one can cite equivalents to almost each one of these expressions in the words of Christ to His Disciples. "You also shall sit on twelve seats judging the

[10]See Bo Rricxr, "Die Verfassung der Urgemeinde im Lichte jüdischer Dokumente." *TZ*, X, 1954, p. 107.

twelve tribes of Israel" (*Matthew* 19:28). "And upon
this rock I will build my Church, and the gates of hell
shall not prevail against it" (*Matthew* 16:18). The
image of the precious cornerstone, which comes from
Isaias (28:16), is likewise employed by Christ; but it
is applied to His own person.

It will be noted that this permits us to make a very
specific point. It has been frequently thought that the
organization of a hierarchy was a secondary considera-
tion in the Church; that it was not a direct concern of
Christ Himself, Who is not supposed to have wished to
establish a religious community, because He believed
—so it was thought—in the imminent end of time. On
the contrary, however, it can now be seen how the
hierarchy organized by Jesus seems to be rooted in the
very milieu in which He lived and, further, how the
idea of establishing this society hardly conflicts with
the idea of the imminent end of time; because the
people of Qumran, who also believed in the imminent
end of time, did establish a formal religious society.
And this likewise proves that the models which inspired
the structure of the Church are not to be sought in the
Hellenic world but in the Jewish milieu of Palestine.

Another feature concerns the disciples that Jesus sent
out to preach His doctrines in the towns and villages.
His recommendation to them is well-known: "Carry
neither purse, nor scrip . . . Into whatsoever house you
enter, first say: Peace be to this house" (*Luke* 10:4-5).
Now we can read the following about the Essenes in
Josephus: "They traveled with nothing except arms to

protect themselves against brigands. In every town someone was especially designated to receive them as guests" (*Wars of the Jews* II, 8, 4). A similar allusion is found in the Gospel. A few moments before Christ is about to be arrested, Peter says to Him: "Lord, behold here are two swords." And Christ replies, "It is enough" (*Luke* 22:38). This does not mean that the disciples of Christ were connected with the resistance movement organized by the Zealots, as Brandon has asserted.[11] Traveling as they were in a country that had plunged into total anarchy, the disciples had to assure themselves of a minimum of security.

Yet, it is not only the structure of the hierarchy that shows the similarities between the religious community established by Christ and that of Qumran A curious text attests to a similarity of the same kind in the organization of the community itself. In the story of the multiplication of the loaves of bread, as recounted by Mark, we see Jesus ordering His disciples "that they should make them all sit down by companies upon the green grass" (*Mark* 6:39). Now the *Manual of Discipline* reads: "The people will march in due order, according to their thousands, their hundreds, their fifties and their tens" (II, 21-22). Doubtless, this was the procedure followed by the people of Qumran, especially during their annual plenary reunions which took place in the month of September. The similarity therefore is striking. It should be added, however, that this hierarchic arrangement is like that of the ancient

[11]*The Fall of Jerusalem and The Christian Church*, p. 103.

people of Israel at the time of the Exodus (XVIII, 21-25). Here again we are led back to a milieu which is more traditional rather than specifically Essenian.

Alongside of these similarities concerning customs, we shall observe that in His discussions with the representatives of the Jewish sects, Pharisees or Sadducees, Christ takes positions that are often akin to those of the Essenes. Thus the *Damascus* or *Zadokite Document*[12] proscribes all kinds of oaths (CDC, XV, 1-3). The same proscription is to be found in the Sermon on the Mount: "But I say to you not to swear at all, neither by heaven, for it is the throne of God" (*Matthew* 5:34). A similar condemnation occurs of the practice of *corban*, that is the false consecration of an object to God in order to avoid giving it to someone else (*Mark* 7:11; CDC, XVI, 13). In all this it would appear that Christ shares the Essenian criticism of the casuistry of the Pharisees. This always leads us back to the same milieu which is opposed at one and the same time to the Pharisees because of their attachment to tradition and to the Sadducees because of their spiritual intransigence. This milieu, however, certainly includes the community of Qumran which was one of its spiritual centers.

A point of resemblance that is particularly interesting is the attitude with respect to divorce, because there is a similarity in the very terms. In the *Damascus Document* (IV, 12-V, 17) we read: "One of the traps is fornication, by marrying two women at the same

---

[12]*The Damascus Document* is generally referred to as *The Zadokite Document* or *Fragment* by European scholars. Tr.

time, even though the *principle of creation* is: male
and female He created them" (IV, 21). And in Mark
we read: "Because of the hardness of your heart
he (Moses) wrote you that precept (a bill of divorce
to put away one's wife). But *from the beginning of the
creation,* God made them male and female" (10:6).
The similarity is so striking that this text is one of those
upon which J. L. Teicher bases his assertion that the
Damascus Document is Judeo-Christian.[13] This is un-
acceptable. But the fact remains that in both cases the
condemnation of divorce as a deviation opposed to the
primal order of creation is the same.

Thus certain aspects of Christ's conduct are not
without their analogies in the community of Qumran.
Must we conclude, then, that Christ had been an Essene, at least for a certain period during His life? On
this point historians are unanimous in asserting the contrary.[14] Nothing, either in the origins of Jesus or in the
social frame in which He regularly lived, compels us to
such a conclusion. The similarities that we have pointed
out are striking, but they are not decisive. And if the
characteristics that we have disclosed are, as a matter
of fact, to be found among the Essenes and the disciples
of Christ, there is nothing to indicate that they were
peculiar to the Essenes. The ecclesiastical calendar is
also found in the book of *Jubilees* and the *First Book of*

---

[13]Jesus' Sayings in the DSS, JSS, V (1954), p. 38. Also see DAVID
DAUBE, *The New Testament and Rabbinic Judaism,* pp. 71-85.

[14]See in particular DUPONT-SOMMER, *Nouveaux aperçus,* pp. 207-
208.

Enoch which surely are not Essenian documents; communal meals or *chabouroth*, moreover, were an ancient custom.[15]

If the comparisons, therefore, rest very much on the surface, the differences in behavior on the other hand are striking. Here I shall cite two main examples of this difference in conduct which particularly impressed their contemporaries.

The Essenes were deeply attached to the observance of the Law. In this respect they were even more meticulous than the Pharisees. Thus they were very strict in their observance of the Sabbath: members were forbidden not only to work on the Sabbath but even to talk about their work (CDC, X, 19); they were forbidden to walk more than a thousand cubits (500 meters) from their homes (X, 21), and also forbidden to prepare any food (X, 22), or pick up rock or dust in a dwelling place (XI, 10). In this connection we are in the possession of a case particularly interesting because it is alluded to in the Gospels. We are familiar with the question posed by Christ to the great scandal of the Pharisees after He had healed a man suffering from dropsy on the Sabbath day: "Which of you shall have an ass or an ox fall into a pit, and will not immediately draw him out, on the Sabbath day?" (*Luke* 14:5). This would mean that an action of this kind was permitted according to the code of the Pharisees. Now such a case is envisaged in the *Zadokite Document* and the answer given there to the question is negative: "If a human being falls into a

---

[15]See GREGORY DIX, *The Shape of the Liturgy*, pp. 87ss.

place of water, he is only to be brought up by using a ladder or a rope" (XI, 16-17). "If a beast falls into a well, nobody is to lift it out on the day of the Sabbath" (XI, 13-14).

Now if we compare the conduct of Christ with respect to meticulous observation of the Law, we note that He takes an entirely opposite position. And He does this on two levels. First, He affirms the primacy of charity over strict observance of the Law, and this scandalizes the Pharisees and, *a fortiori*, the Essenes To cite but one example, let us recall the passage where Jesus is walking across a corn field with His disciples; being hungry the disciples began to pluck the corn and to eat (*Matthew* 12:1). Upon seeing them, the Pharisees say to Him: "Behold thy disciples do that which is not lawful to do on the Sabbath days." And Christ answers them: "And if you knew what this meaneth: I will have mercy and not sacrifice; you would never have condemned the innocent" (*Matthew* 12:7). Charity therefore is prior to legalistic observances. But there is even more here. In fact Jesus adds: "For the Son of man is Lord even of the Sabbath." This is an affirmation of extraordinary significance, the implications of which we shall discuss later.

A second point on which Christ is radically opposed to the Essenes revolves around the conception of legal purity, particularly in regard to meals. One is struck by the scandal Christ provokes when He eats in the company of publicans and sinners. When Magdalen approaches Him, while He is dining at the house of

Simon the Pharisee, Simon says: "This man if he were a prophet, would know surely who and what manner of woman this is that toucheth him, that she is a sinner" (*Luke* 7:39). Now if this gesture scandalized the Pharisees, it was even more scandalous in the eyes of the Essenes. In order to be admitted to their communal meals, one first had to go through a novitiate lasting for a period of two years; and even then each meal was to be preceded by a ritual ablution in the pools that we have discovered and by a change of clothing. From an Essenian point of view, as Lohmeyer has observed, nothing is more revolutionary than the act of Christ breaking bread with the impure, or entering the house of a pagan like the Centurion. We, too, must ponder the meaning of this revolutionary act. It suffices merely to note it to show how the group of Christ's disciples must have provided a distinct contrast to the particularism of the men of Qumran.

Essenian Practices in the Community of Jerusalem

It is impossible to draw a line of demarcation between the evangelical milieu and that of the first community in Jerusalem. As a matter of fact the essential forms of this community, the council of the Twelve Apostles, the Eucharist Supper, and the baptismal rite, go back to Christ Himself; and we have discussed them in their proper place. Nevertheless this organization was still rudimentary and reduced to its essential structures during the lifetime of Christ. It was only when the first Church began to develop that she found it necessary to give herself a more institutional form. And here the comparisons that can be made with the community of Qumran are striking.

Let us first take up the question of hierarchy. The hierarchy of Qumran comprised first of all the Council of Twelve. But below them were inspectors (*mebaq-qer*) who were responsible for limited groups. In the main their duties were to receive new members, to preside over meetings, and to supervise the distribution of goods. Now this strangely resembles those functions that we have seen performed in the first Christian communities by persons who were likewise called inspectors (*episcopes*). Originally the term did not designate the higher degree of the hierarchy, namely that of the Apostles and their successors, but a lower degree. It is a synonym for the word elders (*presbyters*). The difference between the words seems to me to stem from both Essenian and Pharisaic origins. Thus we have a hierarchy of two degrees which recalls that of Qumran.

It must be said further that there are great similarities between their functions. In fact the role of the Christian *episcopos* is exactly that of presiding at meetings, in particular eucharistic meetings. Moreover, he is responsible for the admission of new Christians to the community: it is he who interrogates and baptizes them. Finally his function is best explained by the very control he exercised over the administration of the goods of the community. Hermas, about whose affinities with the Essenes we are quite sure and whom we shall discuss later, writes of the *episcopos* as follows: "They are hospitable men who always extend a warm and open-hearted welcome to the servants of God. They have made of their ministry a perpetual shelter for the poor and widows" (*Sim.* XX, 27:2).

Here a word should be said about the presence of another group in the Christian community, the prophets. This group has sometimes been contrasted with that of the *episcopos* as representing the freedom of inspiration in the face of the authority of the hierarchy. In fact it appears that here again we are in the presence of an extension of Essenism. Josephus makes mention of several Essenes who were prophets. The prophets heretofore fulfilled a role within the community. Their disappearance will be seen, then, not as the end of the inspiration of the Spirit, but more as the end of an institution so linked to the Jewish world that it lost its meaning outside of it.

We have said that the *episcopos* was particularly in charge of the goods and property of the community. This brings to the fore one of the points about the Qumran discoveries which has shed the greatest light on original Christianity. It is known, as a matter of fact, that the *Acts of the Apostles* tell us that the first Christians held everything in common. Now this holding of goods in common and this renunciation of individual property is one of the most characteristic features of Qumran. At the end of his first year a member renounced the free use of his goods, while still preserving his property; at the end of his second year even this property was renounced. The parallelism here extends even as far as the details with respect to the rules. We recall the story in the *Acts of the Apostles* of Ananias and Saphira who, having sold a field, did not declare to the community the full price received. They were subject to a serious punishment, as a result of which Ananias died on the spot. Now we find a case exactly like this in the *Manual of Discipline*: "Anyone who has lied in the matter of his possessions shall be separated from the purity of the community for a whole year." (DSD, VI, 25). It will be noted, however, that this punishment is less severe.

Since we are discussing the discipline of the community, some other striking analogies must be noted. Thus, with respect to the settling of disputes, the *Manual of Discipline* reads: "No one is to bring charges against his neighbor before the Council without first proving them before witnesses." (DSD, VI, 1). Now this is exactly like the Christian legislation as we know it in the New Testament: first one must directly approach the person from whom one desires to obtain justice; if he refuses, the charge will be brought up before two witnesses. And if this is not enough the case is to be referred to the Council of the community.

The requirements for admission to the community also offer interesting parallels.[16] The *Manual of Disci-*

---

[16]See J. DANIELOU, "La communauté de Qumran et l'organisation de l'Eglise ancienne," *RHPR*, XXXV (1955), pp. 105-107.

(PHOTO WEBB RAPHO)

The cliffs at Ain Feskha overlooking the Dead Sea

(PHOTO WEISS - RA-HO)

Ruins of the monastery and Wadi Qumran
with the Dead Sea in the background.

pline tells us that the candidate must first undergo a course of instruction for one year. He is then admitted to the baths of the community. At the end of the second year he is admitted to the common board (DSD, VI, 18-23). It seems that in the very beginning Christians were content with a brief period of catechistic instruction as evidenced by Philip's baptism of the eunuch of Queen Candace (*Acts* 8:27-38). But very soon there is talk of a period of preparation which at one and the same time consists of a course of instruction and periods of fasting.

Yet this is not the most notable aspect of the similarity, because it would then remain purely an external one. What is remarkable is that the very structure of this catechism seems to have been borrowed from the Essenes by the first Christians. The most ancient catechism has come down to us in two works of the second century, the *Didache* and the *Epistle of the Pseudo-Barnabas,* which texts make use of even more ancient material. This catechism is structured on the theme of the two ways, the way of light and the way of darkness: the Angel of Justice is in charge of the first, the Angel of Iniquity of the second. Now it is impossible not to recognize here the structure of the catechism of Qumran, such as is found in the beginning of the *Manual of Discipline* (III, 13-IV, 26). There we read that there are two spirits, the Prince of Light and the Angel of Darkness, and that the ways of these two spirits are opposed the one to the other. This doctrine of the two ways and two spirits appears to be one of the points in which the dependence of Christianity with regard to Qumran emerges most clearly. It should be noted, however, that the Christians subjected this doctrine to an essential modification by opposing the Angel of Darkness not with an Angel of Light, but with Christ or the Holy Ghost.

The structure of the catechism is not the only point in the *Didache* and in ancient Christian rituals which shows a resemblance to the practices of the community of Qumran. Thus in Qumran admission to the community was preceded by formidable oaths committing the candidate to break with the Sons of Darkness and to adhere to the Law of Moses (DSD, V, 8-10). The ancient Christian practice of renouncing Satan and of making profession of faith in Christ seems to copy such oaths closely. But it should be clearly understood that an essential change was effected by the act of joining which was, in fact, a confession of belief in the divinity of Christ. The practice of dressing the newly baptized in a white robe inevitably recalls the description in Josephus of the white garments worn by those who were newly admitted to the Essenian community (Josephus, *Wars of the Jews*, II, 8:7).

The resemblances are just as striking with regard to another aspect of the cult, namely the daily prayers. We learn from a text in the *Manual of Discipline* that the Essenes prayed three times a day, "When the light of the day begins and when it is in the center of its course and when it withdraws to its appointed habitation" (DSD, X, 1). Now the ritual of the *Didache* tells us: "Pray three times a day" (VIII, 3). The three hours are not specified. They might conceivably have been the three hours during which strict observance of the Law required visits to the Temple, namely at three, six and nine o'clock which correspond to the canonical hours of Tierce, Sext and None. But it is much more probable that such prayers were recited in the morning, at noon, and in the evening. Here, then, we are at the origin of the three hours of the office of the liturgy: Lauds, Sexts and Vespers.[17]

In addition to the hours of prayer it will be of interest to note the relation of prayer to light. This is specifically described by Josephus: "Before the sun rises they address traditional prayers to it as if to implore it to rise" (*Wars of the Jews*, II, 8:5). This practice is contrary to the usual Jewish custom of praying in the direction of Jerusalem. It is even formally condemned in *Ezechiel* (8:16). On the other hand it is customary in primitive Christianity. The prayer *ad orientem* forms part of the baptismal rites. It is the origin of the *orientation* of the churches. This is almost certainly due to an Essenian influence as F. J. Doelger has observed.[18] Regarding the origin of this custom in Essenism itself, it may well have stemmed from a Greek or oriental source.

Alongside of the diurnal prayers we also find nocturnal vigils among the Essenes. Each night certain mem-

[17]JUNGMANN, "Altchristliche Gebetsordnung im Lichte des Regelbuches von En'Feshka, *ZKT* (1953), p. 218.
[18]*Sol Salutis*, p. 44. Saint Basil makes an apostolic tradition of the prayer *ad orientem* (*Traité du Saint-Esprit*, 27, *P. G.*, XXXII, 188B).

bers of the community had to read scripture, "Blessing God together" (DSD, III, 7). This is to be found in Christian tradition ever since Hippolytus' *Apostolic Tradition*. It is the origin of one of our matinal nocturnes: "In the depths of the night rise up from your bed and pray. The Ancients transmitted this custom to us. At this hour all the universe is in repose, blessing God. The stars, the trees and the universe are in repose, blessing God. The stars, the trees and the waters are still. The entire army of angels carries out its ministry with the souls of the Just. Thus, those who believe pray at this hour" (35). The entire passage has an Essenian flavor. The allusion to the Ancients marks the antiquity of this practice. This ritual of prayer, which forms a separate part of the *Apostolic Tradition,* has the unmistakable air of being a Christianized Essenian ritual, such as those in the moral instructions of the *Didache.*

It will be noted that these specified hours for daily prayer do not exhaust the practice itself. For the Essenes, prayer had to accompany all the acts of the day: "At the beginning of each of my daily tasks, when I leave or enter the house, when I sit down or when I rise, when I stretch out on my couch, Him do I wish to celebrate." (DSD, X, 13-14). Now in the *Catechisms* of Cyril of Jerusalem we read the following: "Let us make the Sign of the Cross on our foreheads on every occasion, when we drink and when we eat, when we leave our houses and when we return, and when we go to bed and when we get up. Therein lies a great protection (φυλακτηριον)" (P. G. XXXIII, 816 B). The similarity of expression is striking. Moreover, Cyril here is only re-stating traditional turns of phrase.

The liturgy of the week also presents similarities between Christian and Essenian customs. The celebration of Sunday, the Wednesday and Friday fasts correspond to the special days of the sons of Zadok.[19] Of special interest here is the Essenian custom of nocturnal vigils consecrated to the reading of the Bible and to its interpretation, accompanied by liturgical hymns (DSD, VI, 6-8). Here we are at the origin not of private nocturnal prayer at the end of each day, but of vigils celebrated by the entire community, doubtless the vigils of Sunday night and of principal feast days. Now it is known what an important place such vigils held in primitive Christianity. Clement of Alexandria notes that "those who keep nocturnal vigils make themselves like unto the angels called the Watchers" (*Ped.*, II, 9). This is one of the Essenian names for angels (CDC, II, 18; *Enoch*, LXI, 12) and the passage cited is very much in this spirit.

Two facts are noteworthy in regard to the annual liturgy, leaving aside great feast days like Easter and Pentecost—common to all Jews and which we have preserved by endowing them with a new meaning. On the one hand the Essenes held a solemn annual assembly during which members renewed their vows to the ideals

[19]See A. Jaubert, "Le calendrier des Jubilés et les jours liturgiques de la semaine," VT, VII, (1957), p. 60.

of the community (DSD, I-16-19). There is a striking similarity between this ceremony and the annual renewal of the baptismal commitment during the Easter season in the Christian community. In addition—and this is specifically Essenian—the community of Qumran especially celebrated the beginning of each of the four seasons which always falls on the same day, doubtless a Wednesday, given the calendar they used: "On the regular day of each season, from the session of the harvest to the gathering of fruits, from the season of the sowing to that of germination, in short throughout all my life, one law shall be engraved upon my tongue, so that I may sing his praise" (DSD, X, 2-9). Now Father Jungmann has posed the question whether this might not be the origin of the Four-Seasons (*loc. cit.* p. 217).

The dependency of the first Christian community on Qumran for its practices seems to be established on another point too It will be noted that the New Testament and the first Christian writers always cite the same prophets in the Old Testament in connection with Christ. As a result, it was legitimately inferred that there must have existed a collection of such prophecies for the use of preachers and catechists. Moreover we have others that date from the later periods. Such collections must have been very old and even anterior to the New Testament which makes use of them.

Now one of the sensational discoveries of Qumran, to which Allegro in particular has drawn attention, is that of a collection of messianic *Testimonia*.[20] It is

[20]"Further messianic reference in Qumran literature," *JBL*, LXXV, (1956), pp. 174-188.

therefore probable that the Christians borrowed this practice from the Essenes. But there is something even more striking: many of the *Testimonia* texts of Qumran are to be found in the New Testament or in the first Christian writers, such as those in *Amos* (9·11) in particular: "I will raise up the tabernacle of David . . . and I will rebuild it as in the days of old," and *Numbers* (24:17): "A star shall rise out of Jacob." The first of these texts is applied to James during the conversion of the Gentiles "after God had first visited" them (*Acts* 15:14-17). The same text is mentioned in the Qumran scrolls and is applied to the establishment of the community (CDC, VII, 16). And as for the text on the star which is to be found in several of the Qumran fragments (DSW, XI, 6; CDC, VII, 19), it is also a text of which the first Christians were very fond. Two passages in the New Testament seem to allude to it: the star of the Magi and in *Apoc.* (22:16) where Christ is called "the bright and morning star."

More extensive and deeper research would multiply such examples, and show that a number of passages cited in the New Testament were dear to the monks of Qumran. We have already mentioned *Isaias* (40:3 and 28:16), but there are also many others. The text in *Amos*, concerning Judgment Day, has a very important place in the *Damascus Document* (Zadokite): "And I will break the bar of Damascus" (*Amos* 4:5) is applied by this document to the exile of the community to Damascus and cited by Stephen in his speech before the Council (*Acts* 7:43). Zacharias' prophecy that the Lord would "strike the shepherd, and the sheep shall be scattered" (*Zach.* 13:7) refers, according to the *Da-mascus* or *Zadokite Document* (XIX, 8), to the enemies of the community. Christ will apply it to Himself in Mark (14:27): "I will strike the shepherd, and the sheep shall be dispersed."

Explicit citations of or allusions to *Genesis* 49:10 (the scepter of Judah),[21] to *Deut.* 18:18 (the prophet),[22] and to *Isaias* 6·1 (the servant),[23] and 11:1-5 (the scion of David),[24] and 9:6 (the wonderful Coun-sellor)[25] can also be pointed out in the Qumran scrolls. All these texts play a very important role for the very first Christians, because it is through them primarily that they give expression to the great mystery of Christ. This point, without doubt, is one of those where the similarities that we are seeking to disclose are the most striking of all.

There now remains the task of studying the meaning given to these texts, and it is there that differences appear. And they clearly express the contrast between the waiting of the hermits, for whom the Messiah is not yet come, and that of the Christians, for whom He is arrived. We shall return to this matter later.

Thus it would appear evident that the first Christian community is immersed in a Jewish milieu akin to that

[21] *4 QpGen;* ALLEGRO, *loc. cit.*, p. 174, *1 QBen;* Qumran Cave 1, p 128.

[22] *4 Qt;* ALLEGRO, pp.182-183.

[23] *DST,* XVIII, 14; *4 QpIsa; CDC,* XIII, 10.

[24] *4 QT;* ALLEGRO, p. 180 (see also pp. 175 and 176); *1 QBen;* Qumran Cave 1, p. 128.

[25] *DST,* III, 10.

of Qumran from which it borrowed many forms of expression. Seemingly such borrowings even increased. But it is no less evident that the character of the first Christian community does not lie in the details of its organization, but in the absolutely central place held in it by the person of Christ, His death and His resurrection, to the point that it is impossible to imagine a recital of His life which does not center on this point. Is there a parallel to this in Qumran? For the second time we are led back to this central question, no longer in connection with the life of Christ Himself, but with respect to its place in the faith of the community. This is the question that we shall answer now by comparing Christ and the Teacher of Righteousness.

II

Christ and the
Teacher of Righteousness

ONE OF the most extraordinary aspects of the
Qumran discovery is that it has revealed to us the
existence of a personage called the "moré hassedeq,"
the Teacher of Righteousness or the "Right-Teacher"
who incontestably appears to have been a great religious figure. I deliberately say that the Qumran scrolls
have revealed his existence. Strangely enough—and the
importance of this will be discussed later—none of the
accounts of Philo or Josephus which dealt with the
very milieu in which the scrolls have been discovered,
as A. Dupont-Sommer was among the first to point out,
make the slightest allusion to him. Nevertheless, the
1947 discovery is not at all the first such find that has
brought him to our attention. He is, in fact, already
mentioned—and somehow this was hardly noticed—in
a manuscript discovered in Cairo in 1896, the *Zadokite
Document* or *Damascus Document* which has been
identified as belonging to the same collection of manuscripts found at Qumran.

Here there is no question as to whether this personage may have had any direct contact with Christ or
with primitive Christianity, because he did not live at

the same time. The question, therefore, is quite different from the one that we have discussed in the previous chapter.

It is very difficult to determine the exact dates within which to locate his history: here we find ourselves on very shaky ground. We are dealing with a drama involving two personages: a pious priest, and an impious or "wicked" high priest. In the background of this drama is a group from which much must have been expected (but which betrayed these expectations) and the prospect of a foreign invasion. Now, it becomes necessary to search through what we know about the Judaism that existed two centuries before our era for that specific situation to which these given facts correspond.

There are quite a number of such situations. I shall not list all the hypotheses that have been proposed with regard to this chronological question. They have been admirably summarized by Millar Burrows.[1] It may suffice to know that the hypotheses which can be taken seriously stretch from the pre-Maccabean period to the end of the Hasmonean period, that is to say from around 180 B. C. to 60 B. C. In every way, therefore, this Teacher of Righteousness appears on the scene at least a half-century before the birth of Christ.

But another question poses itself which, if not the most exciting, is at least among the most controversial of those that have been aroused by the discovery of the Dead Sea Scrolls. As a matter of fact some exegetes,

[1] *Op. cit.*, pp. 171-217.

impressed by certain similarities between the expressions describing the personage and the history of the Teacher of Righteousness and those in the Gospels referring to Christ, have thought that the Teacher of Righteousness was a sort of Christ *ante litteram*, as it were. Some have said that he was an incarnated divine being, and that he represented himself as a Messiah. Further, some have asserted that he had been crucified by pagan soldiers in the service of the high priest, that he had appeared in the Temple after his death, and that his disciples awaited his return in the "last days" for the last Judgment. All this would constitute an "Essenian myth" which later was supposed to have been applied to Jesus.

Here we are no longer dealing with similarities between methods of organization or patterns of thought. What is in question is the originality of Christianity in its very essence: the person and the mystery of Jesus. Thus the intense interest aroused everywhere by the question that has been posed is understandable. From the viewpoint of sheer curiosity, particularly at the journalistic level, there is a great temptation to make even more sensational something that already is quite sensational in itself. Moreover, the seriousness of the stakes involved risks inciting rationalists on the one hand, and believers on the other, to request the texts themselves. And this is much less easy to do because many are poorly preserved and others difficult to interpret.

Nevertheless, once the first effect of surprise passed

over and the different interpretations were collated, a certain number of conclusions were arrived at by the group of specialists concerned. Certain hypotheses have been definitely eliminated as a result of an objective study of the documents. Other points have been confirmed. Finally, many questions are being disputed at the present time and will be for a long time to come, because the data furnished by the documents is uncertain. As more progress is made in the publication of the material on hand, new elements will undoubtedly be brought forth. All I wish to do here is present, in line with current research and opinion on the Scrolls, that which is true beyond doubt, that which is certainly false, and that which is still subject to discussion.

Is the Teacher of Righteousness a Dead and Resurrected God?

In order to be able to compare the Teacher of Righteousness with Jesus the essential problem is to find out exactly what we know about the former. The greater part of this chapter will be devoted to the study of this problem.

Allegro, who is among those scholars who have pressed the comparison between Christ and the Teacher of Righteousness to the extreme, is sure that "Jesus is much more of a flesh-and-blood character than the Qumran Teacher could ever be"[2] because of

---

[2]*The Dead Sea Scrolls*, p. 159.

Father Daniélou and Father de Vaux
at the entrance to Cave No. 1.

(PHOTO WEISS - RAPHO)

Cave No 1 where the first discoveries were made.
just above the figure can be seen the original entrance.

the greater documentation that we possess concerning Him. The character of the Teacher of Righteousness is infinitely more difficult to grasp, above all if we limit ourselves only to that which, with certainty, relates to him, by disengaging it from the entire halo of suggestions which do not provide a handle for an exact comparison.

Here the basic text is the *Midrash* or *Commentary on the Book of Habakkuk*. The purpose of this work is to show that the prophecies of Habakkuk have been fulfilled in the history of the Teacher of Righteousness. But beforehand—and this is an essential point— it explains that the very message of the Teacher of Righteousness is to announce that the last days predicted by the prophets have arrived: "And God told Habakkuk to write down the things that would come to pass in the last generation, but He did not inform him just when the end of time would come. As regards the phrase, *that he who runs may read*, this designates the Teacher of Righteousness to whom God has revealed all the mysteries of the words of His servants, the prophets" (VII, 1-5). Here is something that is already amazing: the Teacher of Righteousness at first sight appears as a man inspired by God not to announce a new revelation, but to show that the last days announced by the prophets have come to pass.

At this point we shall make three observations. In the first place we have already noted that the consciousness of living in the "last days" was one of the most outstanding characteristics of the Qumran community in general. The text that we have just read

seems to say that such a belief originated with the
Teacher of Righteousness who had been inspired by
God for this purpose. We have likewise seen that this
feature was also characteristic of John the Baptist. Now
we must go even further and assert that on this point
John the Baptist accepts the revelation of the Teacher
of Righteousness and therefore joins his following. This
aspect of the Baptist's message is not original. Finally
we shall note that the method of interpretation which
consists of pointing out the fulfillment of prophecies
in contemporary events, viewed as belonging to the
last days, is common not only to the Teacher of Righteousness and John the Baptist, but also to the Teacher
of Righteousness and Jesus. We shall see wherein the
differences lie. But this point of contact is, nevertheless,
amazing.

The Teacher of Righteousness is therefore a prophet
whose message is to announce the actual arrival of the
"last days." While carrying out his mission, he runs
into violent opposition. It is this conflict that the *Midrash* presents as the fulfillment of the prophecy of
Habakkuk. It refers to the verse: "Behold ye among the
nations, and see: wonder, and be astonished: for a work
is done in your days, which no man will believe when
it shall be told" (*Hab.* 1:5). The *Midrash* comments:
"[This refers] to those who acted traitorously in collab-
oration with the man of lies, because [they paid no
heed to the words of] the Teacher of Righteousness . . .
come from the mouth of the priest in whose heart God
placed [His wisdom] in order to explain the words

of his servants the prophets, and by whom God has announced everything that will happen to His people and to [His congregation]" (II, 1-10).

Thus the words of the Teacher of Righteousness come from the mouth of God, as is the case with the prophets. On the other hand he himself comes from a priestly group, as we know to be the case with all the Sons of Zadok. For having announced his message, that is to say the coming of the last days and the Judgment of God upon the wicked, the Teacher of Righteousness had come into conflict with traitors in alliance with "the man of lies." This personage undoubtedly is to be identified with the "wicked priest" to be discussed later.

There is a more precise identification in V, 9-12. The verse in Habakkuk (1:13): "Why dost Thou look upon traitors, yet keep silent when the wicked devours a man that is more just than he" (I-13), is interpreted thus: "This refers to the 'house of Absalom' and to the people of his party, who kept silent in the face of the punishment of the Teacher of Righteousness and who did not help him against the man of falsehood." Here the house of Absalom refers to a group of Jews, perhaps the Pharisees, who did not support the Teacher of Righteousness. This point is of interest because it establishes that the Teacher of Righteousness had been the victim of a sentence of condemnation, undoubtedly handed down by the high priest and his tribunal, as Elliger suggests.[3]

[3]*Studien zur Habakuk-Kommentar vom Toten Meer*, pp. 53-54.

Now we come to the two passages that have given rise to most of the discussions. The first is the *Commentary on the Book of Habakkuk* (II, 7-8). First it is necessary to quote the passage: "Will not your tormentors suddenly rise? Will not your oppressors come to life? Then you will be their prey. Because you have plundered many nations, all other peoples will pillage and plunder you." Then the text talks about the punishments to be visited upon the wicked. The *Midrash* is mutilated, but it begins thus: "[This refers] to the priest who rebelled" (VIII, 16). Then there is a lacuna, and the text continues, "his punishment by the judgments of the wicked and the horrors of the evils that they inflicted upon him and the vengeance they wreaked on the body of his flesh" (IX, 1-2). Then the commentary speaks of the punishment of the last priests of Jerusalem. Here another verse from *Habakkuk* (2:8) is quoted: "This refers to the wicked priest whom, because of [the evil] he had done to the Teacher of Righteousness and to the men of his party, God delivered to the hands of his enemies who scourged and tortured him because of his wicked way of behaving against his Elect" (IX, 9-12).

The controversial point at issue bears on the passage that follows the lacuna. A. Dupont-Sommer in fact interprets the phrases "the horrors of the evils that they inflicted" and "the vengeance they wreaked on the body of his flesh" in the sense of severe corporal punishment suffered by the Teacher of Righteousness. "This passage," he writes, "quite obviously alludes to the Passion of the Teacher of Righteousness: he was tried, sentenced, and tortured. He suffered in the body of his flesh; without a doubt he was a divine being who incarnated himself in order to live and die as a man."[4] Perhaps the author, who has in other respects given evidence of great perspicacity, would no longer subscribe to this text today. But it is still in circulation, and most attempts to compare Christ with the Teacher of Righteousness are based on it.

It is quite true that the *Midrash* speaks of trials and corporal punishments. But this does not entail the specific description of one being tortured and put to death. Hence, use of the word "Passion" here is incorrect. In addition, Dupont-Sommer speaks of an incarnated divine being, basing his opinion solely on the expression "body of his flesh," as if this meant that the person who is the victim of this ill-treatment has assumed a carnal body because he is a being of a different nature. Now the expression "body of his flesh" simply designates the animal part of man. *Ecclesiasticus* writes: "The debauched man finds no peace in the body of his flesh."

Given the lacuna in the text, it must be added that it is not even certain that this passage refers to the Teacher of Righteousness. It might apply to the "wicked priest" who behaved badly towards the Teacher of Righteousness, here called the Elect. This is why he has been punished by God, as we are told at the end of the passage. But even if the text does refer to the Teacher of Righteousness, it is impossible to see

[4] *Aperçus préliminaires sur les manuscrits de la mer Morte*, p. 47.

more in this than the fact that he was the victim of cruel corporal punishments. Now since it is the *only* text on which the idea that the Teacher of Righteousness was a divine being and that he underwent a Passion is based, it must be said that these two features must be totally eliminated from the person of the Teacher of Righteousness.

The same can be said for a second passage of the *Midrash* where, in connection with the verse (2:15) in the prophecy of Habakkuk: "Woe to him that giveth drink to his friend, and presenteth him gall, and maketh him drunk, that he may behold his nakedness," one may read the following comment: "This refers to the wicked priest, who persecuted the Teacher of Righteousness, in order to confuse him by a show of his ill-temper, desiring to exile him; on their day of rest, the day of Atonement, he appeared among them in order to confuse them and to trip them up, this on the day of their fasting, on the day of their sabbatical rest" (XI, 4-8). The text presents a number of difficulties. It deals throughout with the persecution of the Teacher of Righteousness by the wicked priest. But here the word *glwthw* occurs which can be translated either as "to strip" or "to exile." The second meaning has been adopted by Millar Burrows, Kuhn, and Allegro, and it seems preferable. It excludes the putting to death of the Teacher of Righteousness. As Millar Burrows has noted, the wicked priest wanted above all to reduce him to silence.

But the second part is the most interesting. Dupont-

Sommer translates it as a glorious apparition of the
Teacher of Righteousness after his death: "Thus the
Teacher of Righteousness, shining with a divine light,
himself punishes the criminal city."[5] But we have already said that it does not appear that the Teacher of
Righteousness was put to death. The "divine light" is
a possible interpretation of the verb $yp̄$ which means
"to appear"; but this can also designate any "manifestation" whatsoever, and in itself it does not entail the
idea of supernatural glory.[6] Again, we would like to
emphasize that this is not the issue. The real question
is to know whether the personage who thus manifests
himself is indeed the Teacher of Righteousness. Now
the subject of the preceding sentence is the wicked
priest. It would be much more natural to infer, therefore, that it is still he who is being discussed.

But there is something even more striking. This passage is a commentary on a verse in Habakkuk, a malediction against "him that giveth drink to his friend."
Clearly the commentary must be in line with the meaning of the text which is being commented upon. "Those
who trip up" are the equivalent of "those who get
drunk." Thus, he who causes others to stumble or trip
up is the object of a malediction. This naturally excludes the Teacher of Righteousness. Millar Burrows
is certain therefore that the passage refers to the
wicked priest's surprise interruption of the Feast of
Atonement being celebrated by the Teacher of Right-

[5]*Ibid*, p. 55.
[6]See M. DELCOR, *Essai sur le Midrash d'Habacuc*, pp. 36-37.

*The pantry which contained over one thousand small dishes,
neatly stacked in piles along the walls*

eousness who is he who [expounds the law to] his [Council] and to all those who offer themselves to be enlisted among the elect of [God, practicing the law] in the Council of the community, and who will be saved on the Day [of Judgment]." The preceding sentence contained an allusion to the prophet of falsehood. I shall discuss the *midrashin* of Joshua and Nahum, published by Allegro, later.[8] Finally, there is a *midrash* on the 37th Psalm which speaks of "The Teacher of [Righteousness]," appointed by God, "in order to build a community of His elect for Him."[9]

We are on more solid ground with the *Damascus Document*, of which we now possess many copies; because the Qumran caves have yielded up fragments which have confirmed the hypothesis that the work belonged to our sect. In column 1 we read: "God observed their works and He caused to rise among them a Teacher of Righteousness in order to lead them along the way of His heart." The passage is important for fixing the date of the Teacher of Righteousness. For our purposes it confirms what we have seen of his mission by adding the fact that he no longer appears only as an inspired exegete, but as a guide pointing out a new way. This may suggest that, if not the redactor of the *Manual of Discipline*, the Teacher of Righteousness is at least its inspirer.

[8]"Further light on the history of the Qumran Sect," *JBL*, LXXV (1956), pp. 89-96.

[9]Edited by ALLEGRO. "A newly discovered fragment of a commentary of Psalm XXXVII from Qumran." *PEQ*, LXXXVL (1954) pp. 71-72.

Without doubt it is also the Teacher of Righteousness who is alluded to later in connection with those who "listen to the voice of the Teacher of Righteousness and confess before God: We have sinned" and "who lend their ears to the voice of a Teacher of Righteousness and who do not reject righteous ordinances when they hear them" (XX, 28 and 32). It will be noticed, however, that the Teacher of Righteousness is not specifically referred to in the second sentence. One may question whether reference is being made to the Prophet of whom the *Habakkuk Commentary* speaks or to learned men belonging to the sect. As a matter of fact the *Damascus Document* describes the situation of the community as it was after the redaction of the *Habakkuk Commentary*. Insofar as one can interpret the given facts, it seems very clear that after the events described in the *Midrash*, that is, the persecutions of the Teacher of Righteousness by the wicked priest, the community was exiled to Damascus. The Teacher of Righteousness undoubtedly accompanied them there, but he must have already been dead at the time the document was drawn up. If he is the one discussed in our texts this is so only insofar as his teaching was preserved in the community.

This is confirmed by other passages in the *Damascus* or *Zadokite Document*: "All those who entered into the new Covenant in the land of Damascus, but who went astray and cut themselves off from the well of living waters, will no longer be counted in the Assembly of the people and they will not be inscribed in its register from the day of the disappearance of the Unique Teacher until that day when the Messiah of Aaron and of Israel shall rise" (XIX, 33-XX, 1). The Unique Teacher referred to here is probably the Teacher of Righteousness. There is no mention of when he died, whether before the departure for Damascus or afterwards. But he died around the time the document was drawn up. There is, moreover, a specific reference to this later: "Forty years will elapse from the day of the disappearance of the Unique Teacher until the day of annihilation of the men of war who returned with the man of falsehood" (XX, 13-15).

It will be noted that in the text we have cited there is an allusion to the "Messiah of Aaron and of Israel." This is not the place to discuss the question whether we are here dealing with a single personage or two Messiahs, one a priest and the other a layman. But according to our text it is evident that these Messiahs are being waited for by the community. This text, therefore, is decisive proof that the community did not recognize the Teacher of Righteousness as the Messiah. In the eyes of the community, the ministry of the Teacher of Righteousness marked the beginning of the last days. But these beginnings were only the last stage preceding the coming of the Messiah or Messiahs.

There is another passage in the *Damascus Document* which some scholars consider to be an allusion to the Teacher of Righteousness: "The star refers to the interpreter of the Law who came to Damascus, as it is written: A star shall rise out of Jacob and a sceptre shall spring up from Israel. The sceptre is the prince of the congregation, and when he shall rise he shall destroy all the sons of Seth. These escaped at the time of the first visitation" (XII, 18-21) but "when the Messiah of Aaron and Israel will come ... the remainder will be delivered to the sword which carries out the vengeance of the Covenant" (XIX, 10-13).

But who is this interpreter of the Law, to whom is the prophecy of the "star" applied (*Num.* 24:17)? Is it the Teacher of Righteousness? Everything depends upon the establishment of the date of his death. Such an identification cannot possibly be made by scholars who think that the Teacher of Righteousness was put to death by the wicked priest in 63 B. C. It must be recognized that we are dealing with another personage who must have been the leader of the community during its exile in Damascus. It is to him that another passage may allude: "The well is the Law; those who dug it are those of Israel who went to sojourn in the land of Damascus. The stave (Lawgiver) refers to him who studies the Law" (VI, 4-7). Only because the Teacher of Righteousness was not put to death could one apply the prophecy to him. But in every way the personage who is called "the star" is expressly distinguished from the Messiah of Aaron and Israel, and from the "sceptre" that will pronounce judgment upon the nations and that is expected in the future.

The texts that we have just cited are the essential passages in which the Teacher of Righteousness is explicitly in question. Nevertheless, some are of the opinion that they have come upon allusions to his person and to his mission elsewhere. This raises the question of the interpretation of the *Book of Hymns*, or *Psalms of Thanksgiving*, the *Hodayot*. These constitute perhaps the brightest jewel among the discoveries of Qumran. They are admirable psalms, comparable to some of those in the Old Testament. Their structure is similar, as Mowinckel has shown.[10] The ensemble is a hymn of thanksgiving to Jehovah for having escaped from a great danger. It is possible, as Bo Reicke has suggested in a still unpublished lecture, that these are liturgical texts used during the meetings of the community, at which, according to Josephus, hymns were sung. This, however, does not exclude the possibility, demonstrated by Mowinckel, that they may be personal compositions, relating to particular experiences like certain of the psalms of David.

The question then arises as to whether we can attribute them to a particular author. Here, certainly, sheer conjecture plays a great role.

It is possible that there were several authors and that the collection covers a long period of time. Nevertheless, there is a great similarity throughout in style, thought and feeling. Moreover, the importance attached to these psalms by the community is attested by the fact that one of the hymns, indeed one of the most beautiful, was placed as an annex at the end of the *Manual of Discipline*. Finally, the circumstances they

[10]"Some remarks on Hodayot 39, 5-20," *JBL*, LXXXV, (1956), pp. 265-275.

describe correspond exactly with the trials undergone by the Teacher of Righteousness, but only on the condition of admitting that he was not put to death and that he composed the hymns during his exile in Damascus. This question was first posed by Sukenik, taken up by Mowinckel,[11] and discussed most recently by Henri Michaud.[12] Given the actual state of affairs, it is far from being settled. However, the probabilities in favor of attributing them to the Teacher of Righteousness are at least sufficient to consider these hymns as an expression of his thought.

If this be so, several important conclusions are permissible. First of all the *Hodayot* confirm what the other texts say about the life of the Teacher of Righteousness, which makes their attribution to him even more probable. He had received a mission from God, he had run into opposition, he had been reduced to extreme desperation, but God had delivered him. This is what is shown in column II, 8-19. If these events are really those mentioned in the *Midrash*, then it must be concluded that he was not put to death—a conclusion that is confirmed by the fact that an exile is here in question.

As has been admirably analyzed by Henri Michaud, the most profitable aspect of the *Hodayot* is that they introduce us to the soul of the Teacher of Righteousness. Several characteristics will be noticed. The first one is

[11]*Loc. cit.*, p. 276.
[12]"Le maître de la Justice d'après les Hymnes de Qumran," *Bull. Fac. Theol Prot. Paris,* XIX (1956), pp. 67-77.

the deep humility of the Psalmist. He is aware that he is a sinner. Thus in column I, 22-24, the author declares himself to be "a sink of iniquity, a carcass of sin, a principle of waywardness, perverted, and without understanding." And in column IV, 35-37, he writes: "I remember all my faults and also my infidelities to my fathers. Then I said to myself: Because of my sins I am cut off from Thy Covenant. But upon remembering the power of Thy hand and the abundance of Thy mercies, I rose again." We shall discuss the importance of this characteristic later.

Also admirable is what Michaud calls "his sense of the creaturely condition" and of his nothingness before God. Here the texts recall Job: "Thou hast assigned to man an eternal destiny with the spirits of knowledge, so that Thy name may be praised in joyous song. But I who am made of clay, what am I? A thing kneaded of water, what is my worth?" (col. III, 22-23).

The same accents can be found in the final psalm of the *Manual of Discipline* which seems to have been written by the same author. Of special note here is the author's deep-seated feeling that he possesses naught of his own and that his eternal destiny depends solely upon the grace of God.

In fact, a final characteristic of the author is his sense of the unique majesty that is God's alone. For this reason it has been said that he was a deeply religious being, a great mystic. He attributes all glory to God. "Outside of Thee nothing is wrought; nothing is known outside Thy will. For there is no other person beside

Thee, none whose power rivals Thine" (col. X, 10-11).
His delight is to praise God untiringly, a praise from
his lips which marks the time of day and all the seasons
of the year: "I wish to praise Thy name among those
who fear Thee, by my hymns and psalms of thanksgiving and by my prayers, when daylight first emerges
from its abodes, and during its daily orderly course
through its appointed rounds and in the evening when
begins the reign of darkness" (col. VIII, 4-6). This
sanctification of time was to remain one of the most
characteristic features of the Qumran community.

The Zadokite Use of the Messianic Prophecies

The *Hodayot* also pose a final problem that is not peculiar to them, namely the application of Messianic
terms or texts to the Teacher of Righteousness. In order
to be correctly posed, this problem must be viewed in
relation to the whole collection of Messianic themes
found in the documents. Now, on the basis of what we
have seen until now, two points emerge quite clearly.

First, one of the most remarkable characteristics of
the community is the general application of prophetic
and singularly Messianic texts to its own history. This,
as has been said, attests to the fact that the community
considered itself as belonging to the last days. And we
have also noted the use made of Messianic texts such
as that in *Isaias* 27:16, on the cornerstone, or in *Num.*
24:17, on the star.

A second characteristic appears to be equally certain: the community lived in expectation of the coming of the Messiah. We have pointed out the testimony to this waiting in the *Damascus Document* where it is a question of the coming of "The Messiah of Aaron and of Israel" (CDC, XX, 1). But this is also to be found in the *Manual of Discipline*: "They must conform to the ancient ordinances, by which the men of the community have begun to correct themselves, until the coming of a prophet and the Messiahs of Aaron and of Israel" (IX, 10-11). One of the most important fragments discovered in Cave 1 describes the meals of the community "when God will beget the Messiah."[18] Here again it is a question of both a priestly and a lay Messiah. A fragment found in Cave 4 speaks of waiting for the "Messiah of Justice" who is "the scion of David."

How then does the problem pose itself with respect to the Teacher of Righteousness? It is clear that he is not the Messiah, who is still expected. But on the other hand certain Messianic texts are considered to have been fulfilled. May it not be maintained then that the future Messiah will be a re-appearance or a return of the Teacher of Righteousness? We may ask ourselves whether this hypothesis is not the projection in the Qumran texts of the Christian doctrine of the two *Parousias*. Yet, many expressions can at one and the same time either designate a historical personage or be applied to the Messiah. Clearly the attribution of Mes-

[18]*Qumran Cave I*, p. 117. See R. GORDIS, "The begotten Messiah in the Qumran Scrolls," *VT*, VII (1957), pp. 191-194.

sianic texts would be a fact of great importance. But is this really so? To answer this question we must take a look at the texts.

Allegro bases his opinion on a small fragment of the *Midrash of Joshua* in which the "Lion of Wrath" and the "Last Priest" are in question in the same context. Allegro reasons as follows: If the "Lion of Wrath" is the wicked priest and if it is he who is in question in an eschatological context, this means to say that the "Lion of Wrath" will come in the last days. Hence the "Last Priest" is also the Teacher of Righteousness, returning for the last days.[14] But this is only a tissue of hypotheses Perhaps the "Lion of Wrath" is the wicked priest,[15] but it is evident neither that the "Last Priest" is the Teacher of Righteousness nor that the "Lion of Wrath" must return in the last days. Nothing really can be inferred from this fragment which, moreover, is in a mutilated state.

Other scholars insist on the fact that the same expressions designate the Teacher of Righteousness and the expected Messiah. In a passage of the *Damascus Document*, as translated by A. Dupont-Sommer, the Messiah is designated as "he who will teach righteousness (*yoreh hassedeq*) in the last days" (VI, 11). But what is indeed curious here is that the author avoids using the expression "Teacher of Righteousness" (*moré*

[14]*The Dead Sea Scrolls*, pp. 148-149.

[15]This identification which Allegro draws from the *Nahum Commentary* has been challenged by Rowley, "4 Qp, Nahum and the Teacher of Righteousness," *JBL* LXXV (1956), pp. 188-193.

hassedeq) which is never applied to the Messiah. On the other hand the expression "anointed" does not seem to be applied to the Teacher of Righteousness. And yet in other respects it is repeatedly applied to diverse personages in the history of Israel. In A. Dupont-Sommer's translation of the *Damascus Document* it particularly so designates Zadok, the high priest, twice (CDC, II, 12, VI, 1).[16] Thus the Teacher of Righteousness could very well be called "the Anointed" without thereby being identified as the Messiah. And it is no less true that the fact that the expression is never applied to him might indicate a desire to avoid any confusion between him and the expected Messiah.

We encounter a completely parallel situation in connection with the use of the word "Prophet." The term can designate the eschatological Messiah referred to in *Deut.* 18:18: "I will raise them up a prophet out of the midst of their brethren like to thee." This text forms part of the *Testimonia* of Qumran (4 QT). It has been published by Allegro and seems to refer to the Messiah of the last days in DSD, IX, 11.[17] It likewise forms part of the *Testimonia* of the New Testament where it is applied on four occasions to Christ (*Acts.* 3:22; 7:37; *John* 1:21; 7:40). It is also frequently applied to Christ by a Judeo-Christian sect composed of converted Essenes, the Ebionites, whom we shall discuss later (*Rec. clément;* 1, 36, 43, 56; *Hom. clément* III,

[16] See also *DSW*, XI-7; *DSD*, 11-12.
[17] "Further Messianic References in Qumran Literature," *JBL* (1956), pp. 182-183.

53). It is never applied, for that matter, to the Teacher of Righteousness in the Qumran texts, which seems to be due to the same desire to avoid any ambiguity. This is even more remarkable in that another personage, Dositheus, not without relations with Essenism, albeit of a doubtful kind, does not hesitate to apply the passage from Deuteronomy to himself and thereby pass himself off as the Messiah (ORIGEN, *Contra Celese*, 1, 57). The Teacher of Righteousness seems to be more like John the Baptist, who, in answer to the question, "Are you the Prophet?" answered, "No" (*John* 1:21).[18]

Another expression is that of the "Elect." The Teacher of Righteousness is so designated in the *Habakkuk Commentary* (DSH, IX, 12). Now the word can have a Messianic meaning as in *Isaias* 42:1: "Behold my servant, I will uphold him: my elect, my soul delighteth in him." It is applied twice to Christ in the New Testament (*Luke* 23:15, *I Peter* 4:2). But in the Old Testament it at first designates any man who has been chosen to carry out a particular mission, such as Joshua or Moses. Thus the mere use of the word is not sufficient to designate a Messiah. And, for that matter, it is not at all certain that the word is applied to a Messiah in the Qumran documents.

In fact the only text that can be invoked here is the *Habakkuk Commentary*, 12-13: "These words mean that God will not destroy His people by the hand of

[18]Re this comparison between the Teacher of Righteousness and John the Baptist, see BROWNLEE, John the Baptist in the light of the ancient scrolls, *Interpretation*, IX (1955), pp. 78-86.

the nations, but will place the execution of the judgment of all nations and peoples in the hands of His
Elect" (V, 3-4). The translation I give is A. Dupont-
Sommer's. He comments that "the final judgment will be
executed by the Elect of God, that is to say by the
Teacher of Righteousness." But this interpretation runs
directly into textual difficulties. It should not be read in
the singular, but without doubt only in the plural.
Further down in the same passage, (X, 13) the expression "the elects of God" is clearly plural in meaning.
Here we would be in the possession of an important
doctrine, that of the participation of the saints in the
Judgment, which we will come upon again in the New
Testament. Thus it is highly improbable that the Messiah is meant in this particular text.

The question rises in a similar fashion with respect
to the Messianic prophecies. The Qumran documents
make much use of them, but in a surprising way and
without particular reference to the Teacher of Righteousness. We have already come upon *Numbers* 24:17,
where the star is in question. In the *Damascus Document,* as we have seen, it can be applied to the Teacher
of Righteousness if he had been at Damascus; but if
we follow A. Dupont-Sommer's chronology, it designates his successor instead. We find it again in DSW,
XI, 6. Now here it designates King David; and, as we
know, it will be applied later to the Zealot chieftain, Bar
Kokeba, "the son of the star." The expression "Interpreter of the Law" presents an analogous case. Al-
though there is nothing Messianic about the expression

itself, it seems to apply to the Messiah: 4 QT.[19] Now in the *Damascus Document* it is applied to the leader of the community in the country of Damascus.

The *Hodayot* make much use of the Messianic prophecies of *Isaias*. In column III, 7-10 there is a description of the sufferings of a woman who brings forth "a male child" "an admirable counsellor in all his almighty power." This is probably an allusion to *Isaias* 9:6, as Brownlee, Black,[20] and Dupont-Sommer have noted.[21] and here it is definitely a question of the Messiah. But this Messiah is yet to come. The author of the Psalm identifies himself with the woman, who is the community and not the Mother of the Messiah. Mowinckel[22] has been very specific on this point. The psalmist in no sense identifies himself with "an admirable counsellor in all his almighty power." It is interesting to compare the text with *Apoc.* 12:4, and *John* 16:21.

Other prophecies of *Isaias* are applied to the community. This appears to have been a common practice. Such is the case with the celebrated passage from *Isaias* 11:1, on "a rod out of the root of Jesse." It would seem that column VIII, 7 clearly alludes to it.[23] The most striking case is that of *Isaias* 28:16. The *Manual of Dis-*

[19]Allegro, "Messianic References," p. 176.

[20]"Messianic Doctrines in the Qumran Scrolls," *Stud. Patrist.*, II (1957), p. 449.

[21]"La Mère du Messie et la Mère de l'aspic dans un hymne de Qumran," *RHR*, CXLVII (1955), pp 174-188.

[22]"Some Remarks on Hodayot, 39, 5-20," *JBL*, LXXV (1956) p. 277.

[23]See G. VERMÈS, "Quelques traditions de Qumran," *Cahiers Sioniens*, p. 54.

cipline (VIII, 7) applies it to the community, while Christ applies it to His Person. In column XVIII, 14 the author of the *Hodayot* describes himself with features borrowed from Isaias: God has sent him to bring "cheer to the humble" (*Isaias* 61:1). But this same passage from Isaias serves to describe the duties of the *mebaqquer*, or overseer (CDC, XIII, 10).[24] Brownlee, therefore, is right in not seeing any specific Messianic purpose therein.[25]

A curious case is presented by the passage from *Zach.* 13:7: "Strike the shepherd, and the sheep shall be scattered." We know that Christ applied this text to Himself (*Mark* 14:27). It is cited in the *Damascus Document* (as translated by A. Dupont-Sommer, XIX, 7-9) where once again we can note its particular links with the New Testament in this area. But in this text the shepherd designates the infidel leaders of Israel who will be punished by the judgment of God. This completes the task of showing the extreme liberties that the Zadokites took with Messianic prophecies. Or rather, that which appears constant and which in effect constitutes their essential idea, is the application of the texts to the community. But these texts have no particular link with the Teacher of Righteousness. This will constitute an essential difference with respect to the interpretation of these same texts in the New Testament.

---

[24]"The Servant of the Lord in the Qumran Scrolls," *BASOR,* CXXXV (1954), pp. 33-38.

[25]Bo REICKE, *The Jewish Damascus Document and the New Testament,* p. 17.

A final question is then posed. We possess, in addition to the Qumran documents, numerous texts that are connected with the Judaism of the time of Christ: the *Book of Jubilees,* the *First Book of Enoch* and the *Psalms of Solomon.* Points of contact have been established between these works and the doctrines of Qumran. Better still, fragments of the first two mentioned works have also been found there. Without emanating from the group itself, since they were older than it, these works were adopted by the monks of Qumran Now another text, preserved in Greek with Aramaic fragments, entitled *The Testaments of the Twelve Patriarchs* has been compared to these works. It is certain that there are similarities between this text and the Qumran scrolls.

Among the *Testaments* there is the *Testament of Levi* which contains a remarkable description of the Messiah: "Then the Lord will cause a new priest to rise, to whom all the words of the Lord will be revealed. He will execute a judgment of truth on the earth for a multitude of days. And his star will rise in the sky like that of a king. Under his priesthood sin will disappear" (XVIII, 1-16). A. Dupont-Sommer has attached great importance to this text: "Let me say at once: it seems to me that this new priest . . . is the Teacher of Righteousness himself. . . ."After his earthly career, after his ignominious death, is now to be seen translated to an eschatological plane, invested with full Messianic glory, and enthroned as chief of the new universe, "Saviour of the World . . . eternal Priest."[26]

[26]*The Jewish Sect of Qumran and the Essenes,* pp. 51-52.

In the first place it must be objected that nothing authorizes us to see the Teacher of Righteousness in the personage announced for the last days, Priest or King; the Teacher of Righteousness is a personage of the past and has never passed himself off as a Messiah. It was his disciples, according to A. Dupont-Sommer, who made of him a Messiah. This interests us indeed because it is a recognition that he himself never represented himself as such. But nothing permits us to assert that the expected personage is a manifestation of the Teacher of Righteousness. On the contrary, we have seen that all the documents make a clear and express distinction between him and the Messiah.

But there is still more. The argument put forth by A. Dupont-Sommer is based on the supposition that the text is Essenian or that it stems from the Essenian period. It would have been interesting to know whether any fragments of it were found at Qumran. Two years after the publication of A. Dupont-Sommer's book in 1955, M. Milik, one of the leading archeologists presently working in Jerusalem, published in the *Revue Biblique* fragments of a *Testament of Levi* that had been found at Qumran. Now these fragments have nothing in common with the *Testament of Levi* of the *Testaments of the Twelve Patriarchs*. The fact that it has been impossible to discover such fragments "practically excludes," says Milik, "the pre-Christian or Palestinian origin of the apocrypha. Everything leads to the belief that the *Testaments* are a Judeo-Christian work that made great use of extant Jewish writings" (R.B., 1955, pp. 405-410). This hypothesis, which has always been maintained, has been confirmed anew by a book written by Jonge.[27] Hence it is quite definitely a Christian work in which the description of the Messiah contains unique and distinctive Christian features.

The Grandeur and Limits of the Teacher of Righteousness

At last we are at the end of our long inquiry. This was necessary in order to establish all the points at issue. All that remains now is to draw conclusions. In the first place, the Teacher of Righteousness appears to us as a truly admirable religious figure. And undoubtedly one of the most sensational discoveries of Qumran is the revelation of the existence of one of the great religious figures in the history of humanity. Not only is our curiosity satisfied, but humanity is enriched thereby. The completion of the publication of the discovered documents will allow us to obtain a fuller view and a more precise picture of his character.

Very little is known of his life, and it is difficult to fix exact dates. We know that he came from a circle of faithful priests, that a revelation was made to him, and that he ran into violent opposition, that he was maltreated, and that he was eventually sent into exile. He has, without doubt, left behind hymns in which he gave expression to his religious experience. He seems to have died in a normal way. It is nowhere claimed

[27]*The Testaments of the XII Patriarchs* (1953).

that he appeared to his disciples after his death. He was never the object of a cult. It is nowhere claimed that his return was expected in the last days. It even seems as if he fell into an oblivion of sorts. He had successors who were the leaders of the community which he had founded and which, at the time of Christ, did assume a monastic character.

Two things about the Teacher of Righteousness are remarkable. The first is the depth of his religious experience, his deep humility before God, his painful sense of sin, his admirable confidence in God, his experience of grace, and his acts of grace. But all these attributes would make of him only a great religious figure. There is a second thing even more extraordinary. A revelation was made known to him concerning the fact that the last days proclaimed by the prophets had arrived and that the Messiah was near. He inaugurated a new exegesis of Scripture. Now what is amazing is that this prophecy was verified exactly. Thus between the great prophets of the Old Testament and John the Baptist he emerges as a new link in the preparation for the Advent of Christ: he is, as Michaud writes, one of the great figures of Israel's prophetic tradition. It is amazing that he remained so unknown for so long. Now that he is known the question arises as to what we are to do about this knowledge. It is a question that is posed to the Jews: this great Jew announced the imminent coming of the Messiah some dozens of years before the birth of Christ. Furthermore, the question is put to Christians: how to contest the authenticity of such a message which they claim has been fulfilled? Why does not this message, then, form part of inspired Scripture? This is the true mystery of the Teacher of Righteousness.

But the greater he appears to us when we consider him as a personage in himself, the greater the differences that blazon forth when we compare him to Christ. Undoubtedly there are certain similarities: both had been persecuted by the high priests but this was the common fate of many prophets. Resemblances can even be found in their vocabularies: but it is a question of expressions that reflect the religious idiom of the time. On the contrary, differences are immediately noticeable on the most outward plane. A. Dupont-Sommer has pointed them out in his book on *The Jewish Sect of Qumran and The Essenes*: the Teacher of Righteousness is a priest, Jesus is "the Son of David;" the one is an esoteric teacher, the other a popular preacher; the one avoids all contact with sinners like a contagion, the other, on the contrary, lets them approach Him and welcomes them; finally, the scrupulous legalism of the one contrasts with the astonishing freedom of the other.

It is on essentials that the differences blazon forth. I shall bring them together in my concluding pages. "No text," Millar Burrows has written, "allows us to assert that the Teacher of Righteousness be considered as the Messiah." What some have called the Messianism of the Qumran Scrolls has to do with the important place accorded by the documents to the waiting for the advent, also viewed as imminent, of the Messiah. Now the fundamental assertion of the New Testament is not that the last days have begun, but that the event that will bring them to pass has been accomplished with the coming of Christ Who declares that He is the Messiah and that with Him the Kingdom of God has arrived, the Judgment fulfilled, the Resurrection present, and the gates of Heaven opened.

In the second place another fundamental assertion of the New Testament is concerned with the death and the Resurrection of Christ. The good tidings is not that the Messiah is about to arrive, but that Christ is risen. Now it is almost certain that the Teacher of Righteousness did not suffer a violent death, and it is absolutely certain that it is nowhere claimed that he was resurrected. Moreover, even should it be admitted that he was put to death, it is nowhere asserted that his death had a redemptive value. What matters with the Teacher of Righteousness is his message; with Christ, what matters is His work of salvation.

In the third place, one of the most remarkable characteristics of the Teacher of Righteousness—if we grant that he is the author of the *Hodayot*—is his deeply-rooted sense of being a sinner and his desire for purification. In this he recalls the most beautiful Psalms of the Old Testament, in particular the *Miserere*. Now, as has already been observed, one of the most extraordinary characteristics of the person of Jesus Christ is that in Him one never finds the slightest feeling of being a sinner. And this not only in explicit phrases:

"Who among you will accuse Me of sin?" but in the
very character of His behavior. If, moreover, the sense
of sin is the distinctive trait of truly religious figures so
that its absence is always suspect, its absence in Jesus,
in whom everybody recognizes an incomparable religious quality, is an extraordinary enigma.

Fourthly, another characteristic that we have
pointed out in the Teacher of Righteousness is his consciousness of the infinite distance that separates him
from God. Nothing else gives his words such a deep
religious resonance. Now if there is one point that is
certain in the story of Christ it is that He claimed divine
prerogatives, not only by His words but by His entire
behavior. Outside of this the Gospel is inexplicable.
In fact it was because of such affirmations that He was
accused of blasphemy and finally condemned. "Who
except God alone can remit sins?" said the Pharisees,
thereby testifying that in their eyes the action of Christ
remitting sins was equivalent to claiming divine
authority, a pretension which, being made by a man,
was the greatest crime in the eyes of the Jews. It is the
very opposite of the attitude of the Teacher of Righteousness. Nothing more than this attests to the fact
that Christ thereby asserted His divine nature.

Lastly, not only is the first Christian community
centered around the death and resurrection of Christ,
as the fundamental event in all history, but it makes
Christ the object of its cult by bestowing upon Him the
divine title of *Kyrios*. Now in no wise can we see how
the actions or person of the Teacher of Righteousness

might have had a similar status in the Essenian community. Cullman has observed that Philo and Josephus were able to give a complete account of the Essenian doctrine without even mentioning the Teacher of Righteousness. One simply cannot imagine something like this with respect to the Christian faith. Moreover, the very idea of a cult dedicated to the Teacher of Righteousness in Qumran is highly improbable. He is but a prophet honored after his death. He is the support, not the object, of faith.

Such are the conclusions that emerge after a study of the facts. There is still the problem of the Teacher of Righteousness. But it is necessary to leave it where it is. It is extraordinary in itself. It consists of the discovery of a new link in the preparation of the coming of Christ. This will require mature reflection from exegetes and theologians. But one falsifies the problem when one transposes it to the level that purports to establish an equivalence between the Teacher of Righteousness and Christ. The Teacher of Righteousness is one of those who, before John the Baptist, prepared the coming of Christ. But like John the Baptist himself, even if he is very great among the sons of woman, the smallest child of the Kingdom of God is greater than he. This point having been established, it remains our task to study the multiple aspects of the Essenian influence on the authors of the New Testament and on the first ecclesiastical writers.

III

The First Developments
of the Church and the
Community of Qumran

A PRIORI, contacts between Christianity and Essenism were historically and geographically possible during the period following the period that we discussed earlier. We know as a matter of fact that the Zadokite community remained in Qumran up to 70 A.D., as is proved by the coins uncovered there. Now the period from 35 A.D., to 70 A.D., is precisely the period of the first developments of Christianity. In Josephus, the historian, we have a particularly valuable contemporary witness of this period in the history of the Essenes. Josephus at one time was an Essene, as he himself testifies. He dedicated three important accounts to the community. Now one detail that he provides is of great interest: namely, that outside of Qumran itself, many Essenes were scattered throughout Palestine. It was not necessary, therefore, to go to Qumran to find them.

In 70 A.D., moreover, the Romans conquered Jerusalem and Palestine. Many Essenes were massacred, according to Josephus (*Wars of the Jews*, II, 8: 10). It was at this time that the survivors hid their sacred books in the caves, where they have been only recently discovered, and then escaped. Where did they go? They had already been exiled to Damascus around 60 B.C. It is therefore very probable that some of them went there in order to look for members of the community who had remained in Damascus. But it is possible that they also went to other places: the *Hymns* seem to say that the Teacher of Righteousness had gone to Egypt, and Philo, during this Christian era, had known some monks in Egypt, the Therapeutes, who have many points in common with the Essenes. It is quite possible, therefore, that some found refuge there.

Thus it seems that before 70 A.D., and above all after that date, there were Essenes in Syria, Egypt and doubtless even in Asia Minor. These were the very regions where the Christian missions developed, concentrating especially on Jewish circles. Information about primitive Christianity in Egypt is scattered; but it is known that Paul was in Damascus and in Asia Minor, and John in Asia Minor. During the period that interests us today, contact between Essenes and Christians could have taken place not only in Palestine but elsewhere. This was quite probable both geographically and historically. A study of the available facts shows this to be certain beyond doubt. And it is equally beyond doubt that, during this time, the contacts were closer and the Essenian influences more striking.

Essenes and Hellenists

The first disciples of Christ, in particular the Apostles, were not Essenes. The only one in connection with whom such a question might arise is the Apostle John; he might have had some contact with Essenes before becoming a disciple of John the Baptist. The others came from a totally different social group: Gallileans in the main, they did not belong to priestly families. Peter was married—his mother-in-law was healed by Jesus—and James was a cousin of Jesus about whom, we have said, there was nothing Essenian. Among the Jewish groups of that time the one to which they probably belonged was that of the Zealots, Jewish messianists, who to a great extent were recruited among the common people of Gallilee. Cullman has observed that Judas Iscariot doubtless means Judas the brave, the resistance fighter.[1] This may also be true of Peter and of his brother Andrew.

But were there not any Essenes who were converted later? We can be certain of this, even though it is difficult to identify them. In chapter six of the *Acts of the Apostles* we learn that a great company of priests had been converted. These priests constitute a group known as the Hellenists. The meaning of the term has given rise to a polemical discussion. Were they Jews who spoke Greek? Cullman thinks that it was their way of life rather which distinguished them from other

[1]*Christ et César*, pp. 18-19.

Hebrews.[2] But all this remains very strange. Later Justin, when enumerating the Jewish sects, will speak of Sadducees, Helleniens, Pharisees and Baptists (*Dial.* LXXX, 4). Certainly, the Essenes who are in question were a purely Jewish sect.[3] Now the absence of the Essenes in this list leads one to ask whether the Essenes may not be those designated as Helleniens. On the other hand there is a temptation to compare these Helleniens with the Hellenists mentioned in the *Acts*. This constitutes a primary argument in favor of viewing the latter as Essenes.

Is it possible for us to know something about these converted priests? The answer is yes because there is one of them who is particularly famous: the deacon Stephen whose long defense speech is contained in *Acts* 7:1-53. This speech, as Cullman has pointed out, presents startling similarities with one of the Essenian manuscripts, the *Damascus Document*. The theme of this speech is to show that the Jews have not ceased to be infidels, despite the prophets whom God had sent to them. This is also the theme of an exhortation in the *Damascus Document* (II, 14, III, 12). But there is something even more specific. Stephen says that an angel appeared to Moses, established him as a leader of his people and ministered to him (*Acts* 7:30-36). Now the *Damascus Document* also says that Moses received his authority from an angel (V, 18). Stephen cites a

[2]"The significance of the Qumran texts for research into the beginnings of Christianity," *JBL*, LXXIV (1955), pp. 220-221.

[3]See M. Simon, "Les sects juives chez les Pères de l'Eglise," *Stud. Patr* (1957), II, pp. 535-537.

very strange text of Amos: "And you took unto you the tabernacle of Moloch, and the star of your god Remphan" (*Acts* 7:43). This text is also cited by the *Damascus Document* (VI, 14-15). Finally Stephen tells of the persecutions of the Jews directed against those who prophesied "the coming of the Just One" (*Acts* 7:52). Here one may ask whether he is not dealing with the persecutions suffered by the Teacher of Righteousness.

If, along with Cullman, we can identify these Hellenists as converted Essenes, the consequences should prove interesting. In fact we do know that these Hellenists were driven out of Jerusalem because of their attitude with regard to the Temple. Exiled, they became the first Christian missionaries. Samaria was the first region evangelized by them. And from Samaria they were to go to Syria and to Damascus especially. In Damascus, perhaps they found some Zadokites who had remained there ever since their exile, and they probably won some converts among them. In any case it must be pointed out that these Syrian Christians can be more particularly linked to the *Damascus Document* than to the Qumran scrolls. This is an interesting fact that deserves some emphasis.

Dositheus and the Origin of Gnosticism

Before all else, one point should hold our attention. In the course of their mission in Samaria, the Hellenists came into contact with Simon the Sorcerer, who is the father of gnosticism. This movement is characterized by a rigorous cosmological dualism which assigns the rule of the actual world to an inferior god, the demiurge, and which maintains that the true God will come to deliver those who belong to Him in order to usher them into a new world. Simon is the first known representative of this doctrine. His disciples, Satornil and Carpocrates, were to bring it to Antioch; and his disciple, Basilides, to Alexandria. The doctrine was further developed in Egypt by Valentine and his disciples. Up to now, all we know about them comes from the accounts of the heresiarchs. A sensational discovery in Nag Hammadi in Egypt has revealed the existence of a library containing three *codices*, not yet published, but about which H.-Ch. Puech and G. Quispel have furnished valuable information.[4] This movement was to continue in Manicheism which would make a world religion of it, stretching from Turkestan to North Africa, and which would persist up to the Middle Ages among the Cathari and the Albigenses.[5]

The origin of this movement has been one of the most passionately discussed problems for the past fifty years. Some scholars, following Festugière, have tried to link it to Platonic dualism; while others, following Reitzenstein, have tried to link it to the ancient religions of Egypt and Persia. But none of these attempts at a solution of the problem has gained universal acceptance. More recently Quispel has suggested that

[4]Puech, Quispel, Van Unnik, *The Jung Codex*, 1955.
[5]G. Quispel, *Gnosis als Weltreligion*, 1953.

Column 1 of the Manual of Discipline

(PHOTO WEISS - RAPHO)

Pottery, lamps and coins found at Qumran

gnosticism may be linked to the heterodox currents of Jewish thought.[6] As a matter of fact it is striking to see how many elements of gnosticism do derive from Judaism. But in such a case its specific element, that is, its dualism, remains unexplained. Now the Qumran scrolls show us that there was a current within Judaism in which dualism was very marked, since the world was divided between two opposing princes.

Do we have reason to believe in a contact between Simon the Sorcerer and the Essenes? The answer again is yes because Simon was the disciple of a certain Dositheus who clearly seems to have been an Essene. He is introduced to us as a son of Zadok (*Rec.* I, 54). He lived in Kokba, near Damascus, which seems to have been the habitation of Zadokite exiles to the country of Damascus.[7] He was a strict observer of the Sabbath (Origen, *Princ.* IV, 3:2). And he was an ascetic (Epiphanius, *Pan.* XIII). He had known John the Baptist. Further, he applied to himself the text in *Deut.* 18:15, on the Prophet announced by Moses, which is cited by Stephen (*Acts* 7:37) and which, in addition, forms part of the *Testimonia* of Qumran (Qc, I, 121).[8] Later Simon was to separate from Dositheus in order to establish a new sect, the Heleniens. This term greatly resembles the term

[6]"Christliche Gnosis und Jüdische Heterodoxie," *ET* (1954), pp. 1-11.

[7]B. Z. Lurie, "Histoire de la communauté juive de Damas," *Eretz Israel* (1956), pp. 111-118.

[8]A. M. Wilson, "Simon, Dositheus and the DSS," *ZRGG*, IX (1957), pp. 21-40.

Helleniens which, in addition, designated Essenes, whether they were Jews or converts to Christianity. It is therefore very possible that gnosticism, through Simon, may be a radical exaggeration of the Essenian dualism, perhaps as a result of Persian influences. In this case one of the greatest enigmas of the history of religion is on the road to being solved.

Traces of Essenian Thought in St. Paul

But let us return now to the *Acts of the Apostles*. As Stephen was being stoned, a young Jew stood guard over the clothes of his executioners He was called Saul. He had no reason to feel any sympathy for Stephen, because he not only detested the Christians but also belonged to a different Jewish sect than the one of which Stephen was a member: he was a Pharisee. Is there no reason, therefore, to find in him some elements borrowed from the doctrines of Qumran? If some are to be found it would mean that he came into contact with the Essenes after his conversion. Now the fact is that his thought does present characteristics that relate it in a most striking way to those of the Qumran scrolls. This immediately gives rise to a historical question: just when did Paul familiarize himself with Essenism?

It would appear that this contact must have taken place immediately after his conversion. As a matter of fact all the Epistles bear traces of Essenian influences and they are linked to the fundamental themes of the

Pauline correspondence. Hence one hypothesis immediately comes to mind. Paul was converted in Damascus; it was there that he received his first instruction. It was then, doubtlessly, that he came into contact with some Christians who had emerged from Essenism, and who had been converted by the first Christian missionaries who were none other than our Hellenists. It is quite probable, therefore, that Paul may have been instructed in Damascus by these converted Essenes

To be sure, the basis of Paul's faith is purely Christian: it was the risen Christ who revealed Himself to him in Damascus. But it is unquestionable that he presents this faith in a form that frequently recalls Qumran.[9] This is immediately apparent in many expressions. St. Paul writes: "But we have this treasure in earthly vessels" (2 *Cor.* 4:7). Now in the *Hodayot* we read: "I give thanks unto Thee, O Lord, Thou hast done wonders with dust and Thou hast worked powerfully with a vessel of clay" (XI, 3). Paul writes: "Giving thanks to God the Father, who hath made us worthy to be partakers of the lot of the saints in the light" (*Col.* 1:12); and the *Manual of Discipline* reads: "God gave them a heritage partaking of the lot of the saints" (DSD XI, 7).

Certain resemblances go even further and bear on the doctrines themselves. We shall note that Paul associated the notions of mystery, revelation and knowledge: ". . . according to revelation, the mystery

[9]See W. Grossouw, "The DSS and the New Testament," *SC*, XXVII (1952), pp. 1-8.

has been made known to me, as I have written above in a few words. As you reading may understand my knowledge in the mystery of Christ" (*Eph.* 3.3-4). Now nothing in the Qumran documents is more familiar than this conception. Thus in the *Habakkuk Commentary* it is a question of the Teacher of Righteousness "to whom God made known all the mysteries of the words of His servants the prophets" (VII, 4-5). Likewise in the *Manual of Discipline* (XL, 5) we read: "His marvelous mysteries have illuminated my heart," and finally in the *Hodayot* we come upon: "I give thanks unto Thee, O Lord, for Thou hast let me know Your wondrous mysteries" (VII, 26). It will be noted that the conception of knowledge as a revelation of divine secrets is to be found in the Judaism of the times. But this was a very marked tendency at Qumran. It permits us to show that Paul's *gnosis* in every way is purely Jewish.

Two features of this *gnosis* must be pointed out. First is the doctrine of justification. All the authors, Millar Burrows, Grossouw, Braun, are agreed, on stressing similarities with respect to this point. Many aspects of it are common to Paul and the Qumran scrolls. To begin with, there is a personal sense of sin, much more marked than in the Old Testament and which we have already noted. "Man is steeped in sin from birth; justice and righteousness belongeth not to him" (DST IV, 25-27). This sin is not personal, but primordial. Only God can justify it: "In His justice He will purify me of human contagion" (DST IV, 33).

This notion, original in relation to the Old Testament, does not stem from Pharisaism which is based on the works of the Law. Paul therefore must have got it from the doctrine of Qumran.

This doctrine of justification is tied to faith by Paul. And we know that he bases himself on a verse from *Habakkuk* (II, 4): "But that in the law no man is justified with God, it is manifest: because the just man liveth by faith" (*Gal.* 3:11). It would certainly be exciting to find the same verse commented upon in the *Habakkuk Commentary*. Now the fact is that it is commented upon and we read: "But the righteous will live by faith. This refers to all those who observe the Law in the House of Judah which God will spare from Judgment on account of their sufferings and their faith in the Teacher of Righteousness" (VIII, 1-3).

The comparison is striking, but the difference between them immediately blazons forth. In the one case faith is opposed to the Law and in the other it is linked to the Law. Faith in Christ, as Cullman has ably shown, is faith in His redemptive action which fulfills what is impossible for the Law.[10] Faith in the Teacher of Righteousness, on the contrary, is faith in him who teaches how to fulfill the Law. It would almost seem as if this were a Pauline polemic against the *Midrash*.

Another doctrine, indeed the most characteristic of Qumran, also appears in St. Paul with details of expression that leave no doubt as to its origin: it is that of the struggle between the Light and Darkness. Thus in

[10]*Loc cit.*, p. 217.

Romans 13:12, we read: "The night is passed, and the day is at hand. Let us therefore cast off the works of darkness, and put on the armour of light." And in 2 *Corinthians* 6:14, the expression: "What fellowship hath light with darkness? And what concord hath Christ with Belial?" makes of Belial the Prince of Darkness. Now this name which is found only here in the New Testament was one frequently used at Qumran (CDC IV, 13). Another expression, "the Angel of Satan," is found once in 2 *Cor.* 12:7, and in CDC, XVI, 4. Kuhn has likewise pointed out that the list of the works of darkness and the works of light (*Ephesians* 4:17, 5:14) recalls the expressions in the *Damascus Document* (IV, 3) that ring with an amazing similarity.[11]

This similarity appears fully in a passage of the *Acts of the Apostles*, in which Grossouw sees the most astonishing literary parallel with the *Manual of Discipline*. The passage deals with the speech that Paul makes in the Caesarea before a court presided over by King Agrippa and his sister Berenice. Paul tells of the vision he saw on the road to Damascus. These are the words he puts into the mouth of Christ: ". . . Now I send thee to open their eyes, that they may be converted from darkness to light, and from the power of Satan to God, and that they may receive forgiveness of sins, and a lot among the saints by the faith that is in Me" (*Acts* 26:17-18). All these formulas have their

[11]"Die in Palästina gefundenen hebraischen Texte und das N. T.," ZKT (1950), pp. 192-211.

equivalent in the Qumran scrolls, from "open their eyes" up to "a lot among the saints".[12] Now this speech concerns the conversion of St. Paul in Damascus. It is the explanation of his first experience with Christianity. It is also a kind of synthesis of the way in which Christianity appeared in its very beginnings. And if we note in addition that the schema of this speech is entirely Essenian, how can we avoid the thought that it is an echo of the first instruction that Paul received in Damascus, and that in it we have an elementary catechism of sorts? Moreover we have already observed that the structure of the first Christian catechism, such as we find it in the *Didache,* is based on the two ways, that of light and that of darkness. This would appear to provide final confirmation that the Christianity which St. Paul found in Damascus was the Christianity of converted Essenes. And this explains how the very structure of his message presents so great a similarity with that of the Essenes.

St. John and the Theology of Qumran

If the thought of St. Paul shows curious points in common with that of Qumran, the Johannine writings show even more, as has been pointed out by Braun, Albright, Kuhn and Grossouw. These relationships, however, are to be explained by different reasons. In fact, it seems that John may have had several occasions to know the

[12]See GROSSOUW, *loc. cit.,* p. 6.

Essenian group. For one thing he was a disciple of the Baptist and, therefore, could have known the Essenes before becoming a disciple of Jesus. He belonged to the first Christian community in Jerusalem and his contacts with Essenism may, therefore, be explained further by his membership in the original Christian group which we have already discussed. Later he entered into close relations with the Hellenists of Damascus. And finally we shall see that, in Ephesus, he met many Essenian priests who had been driven out of Palestine after 70 A.D.[13]

The similarities between the Qumran scrolls and the *Apocalypse* seem to be linked to the contacts between John and the Hellenists. They revolve around certain details. One senses, for example, that John is familiar with the Messianic *Testimonia* of Qumran and especially those of the *Damascus Document*. Alongside the theme of the stars (*Apoc.* 2:28; CDC, VII, 19) which comes from *Numbers* 25:17, is found that of the rod which refers to the same text in *Numbers*: "... who was to rule all nations with an iron rod" (*Apoc.* 12:5). Also of interest in this connection is 19:15-21 of the same book. Now the *Damascus Document* writes: "The rod is the prince of the community, and when he comes he shall beat down all the sons of devastation." In the same passage of the *Damascus Document*, *Zacharias* 13:7 is quoted: "Awake, O sword." It is applied to the Messiah (CDC, XIX, 10). Now the *Apocalypse* reads:

[13]Braun, "L'arrière-fond judaique du IV Evangile et la communauté de l'Alliance," *RB*, LXII (1955), pp. 43-44.

"And out of his mouth proceedeth a sharp two-edged sword; that with it he may strike the nations" (19:15). This can also be compared to the following verse in the collection of *Benedictions* from Cave 1 (V, 2, p. 29): "Thou strikest the peoples by the breath of Thy word and by the breath of Thy lips wilt Thou dispatch the wicked." These texts allude to *Isaias* 11:14: "And he shall strike the earth with the rod of his mouth, and with the breath of his lips he shall slay the wicked."

It will be noted that in the same passage of the *Damascus Document*, *Ezekiel*, 9:4, is cited. This is the text about the mark on the foreheads of the members of the community of Qumran. It is difficult to determine whether this is taken in a figurative sense or whether it corresponds to a rite. Now the same text is cited in the *Apocalypse*. "Hurt not the earth, nor the sea, nor the trees, till we sign the servants of God on their foreheads" (7:3). After this there follows the celebrated enumeration: "*Ex tribu Juda duodecim millia signati.*" And further it deals with those "who have not the sign of God on their foreheads" (9:4).

Perhaps here we are at the source of a very ancient Christian tradition, namely that of marking the forehead with a cross. It seems clear that the cited text from the Apocalypse signifies that the Christians were marked by the sign of God, announced by Ezekiel. Ezekiel tells us that this sign had the form of a *Tau*, and we know that at that time *Tau* was written in the form of a Latin cross, or Saint Andrew's cross. Now among the very ancient Christian rites of Baptism there exists also that of marking the forehead of the catechumen, who is thereby introduced into the company of the people of God. It is very probable that this is the rite of which St. John speaks. But in this case the sign would originally designate the Name of God of which *Tau* was the expression.[14]

Moreover we can find in Hermas, an ancient Christian writer influenced by Essenism, the expression "to be marked by the Name," while we never come upon the expression "marked by the sign of the cross." It would seem, therefore, that later the sign was interpreted as designating the cross, while originally it was a sign of consecration to the Name of God. And we know that in primitive Christianity "the Name of God" was the expression then current for designating the second person of the Trinity. Since then the mark on the forehead, at baptism, designates consecration to Christ.

On the other hand its does not seem impossible to me that the name of Christian, given for the first time to the disciples of Christ at Antioch, may be an erroneous interpretation of the sign *Tau* which was marked on the forehead and which, as we know, may have had the form of the so-called St. Andrew's cross. Because the form of this cross was the same as the Greek X, the Greeks who did not understand the meaning of the sign might have interpreted it as the first letter of Christos (Χριστος). The interesting feature of this

[14]See J.-L. TEICHER, "The Christian Interpretation of the Sign X in the Isaiah Scroll," *VT*, V (1955), pp. 189-198.

observation should not escape us. For if the Christians inherited the idea of marking the forehead with the sign *Tau* from the people of Qumran then it follows that one of the still-existing rites of the baptismal ceremony originated with them. There is nothing startling about this, however, if we recall having already noted that other rites accompanying baptism, in particular the renunciation of Satan, seem also to trace back to them.

We have observed further that the same passage of the Apocalypse which mentions the signs on the foreheads of the servants of God also lists the number of tribes which make up the people of God. This provides an orientation for us with respect to another writing which we have not yet discussed, but whose relations to the Apocalypse are startling: the *War of the Sons of Light and the Sons of Darkness*. It deals with an apocalyptic struggle between the servants of God and the servants of Belial, which immediately recalls the very theme of the Apocalypse. Moreover the work is specifically composed of long listings of different sections of the army of the Sons of Light. But there are still other startling resemblances to be found in it. The *War* tells us in fact of the "day appointed for tripping up the prince of the realm of perdition and the sending of an angel for this purpose, Michael, whom he has made full of glory so that he can exercise his power" (XVII, 5-6). Now the Apocalypse shows Michael and his angels fighting the dragon: "And that great dragon was cast out, that old serpent, who is

called the devil and Satan . . . I heard a loud voice in
heaven saying . . . now is come salvation . . . the
kingdom of our God, and the power of his Christ"
(12:7-10). It will be noted, but this is an immense
difference, that the power which in Qumran is exercised
by Michael (XVII, 8) is transferred to Christ in the
Apocalypse.

If these similarities with the *Apocalypse* revolve only
around a few details, the relationship between the
Qumran scrolls and the Gospel and Epistles is based on
certain common features. As is known, the Gospel of
John is entirely constructed on the theme of the conflict between light and darkness. This is made clear in
the very first lines: "In him was life, and the life was
the light of men. And the light shineth in darkness, and
the darkness did not comprehend it" (*John* 1:4-5).
Now this is nothing else but the *leitmotif* of Qumran.
We could explain it by the similarity of imagery. But
there also exist similarities of detail so that many
singular expressions whose original background up to
now has been sought here and there, in Hellenism,
among the Mandeans and the Gnostics, now seem to
have found their literary place of origin. This is a discovery of capital importance which shows that the
backdrop of John's thought is Jewish, and thereby a
breach is made in the theses put forth by the two most
important recent commentators on John: Dodd, who
interprets him as stemming from Hellenism; and
Bultmann, who links him to the Gnostics. As Albright
has stated, the debate on the original background of

the Gospel of John appears to be definitely closed.[15]

Let us give some examples of these Essenian atavisms. We find "the children of light" (*John* 12:36) who are mentioned in the *Manual of Discipline* (I, 9; III, 24). But they were already mentioned in *Luke* (16:8) and in the *Epistle to the Thessalonians* (5:5). On the contrary the expressions peculiar to John are "light of life" (*John* 8:12) which is also in the *Manual of Discipline* (III, 7), the expression "he that walketh in darkness" (*John* 12:35) which is in the *Manual of Discipline* (III, 21), "he that doth truth" (*John* 3:21) which is in the *Manual of Discipline* (III, 21), and finally the expression "works of God" (*John* 6:28) which is in the *Manual of Discipline* (IV, 4). The following passage from the *First Epistle of John* is also very characteristic: ". . . Believe not every spirit, but try the spirits if they be of God: because many false prophets are gone out into the world. By this is the spirit of God known. Every spirit which confesseth that Jesus Christ is come in the flesh, is of God. And every spirit that dissolveth Jesus, is not of God: and this is Antichrist" (4.1-3). The idea of distinguishing between spirits is characteristic of Qumran (DSD, V, 24). The same is true with the idea of the Antichrist. But it will be noted that the distinctive characteristic of the good spirit is to recognize in Jesus the Word become flesh. Here too it would appear that

[15]"Recent Discoveries in Palestine and the Gospel of John," *The Background of the New Testament and His Eschatology*. 1956, p. 167.

there may have been some discussions with the Essenes Hence the question may be asked whether John does not place the Teacher of Righteousness among the false prophets.

And in fact, for John, the struggle between light and darkness is not the struggle between Michael, the Prince of Light, and Satan. It is the Son of God who rises to struggle against Satan, "the Prince of this world," as John designates him in accordance with an expression that is distinctively Essenian. Thus, even if the central schema is the same, one of the protagonists changes It would seem that John addresses his gospel to a group familiar with this theme of a conflict between light and darkness, but which radically modifies its content by replacing the "Angel of Light" with "the Word become Flesh." Now who could this group have been but a group of converted Essenes, albeit heterodox, who were driven to Asia Minor by the persecutions of the year 70 A. D.?

A particularly interesting point has been raised by Braun.[16] In the fourth chapter of the Gospel of John, dealing with the woman of Samaria, there is a discussion about Jacob's well which appears as a symbol of the Jewish Law. In fact the Samaritan woman says: "Art thou greater than our father Jacob, who gave us the well, and drank thereof himself, and his children, and his cattle?" (4:12). Now the first text in which the well appears as a symbol of the Law is in the *Damascus Document*. The idea is repeated several times: "The well in question is the Law. Those who dug it are those

[16]*Loc cit.*, pp 24-26.

of Israel, and were exiled to the land of Damascus"
(VI, 4-5). Later mention will be made of "Those who
entered into the new covenant in the land of Damascus
but then turned away from the well of living waters"
(XIX, 33-34). It would appear, then, that when Christ
answers: "If thou didst know the gift of God, and who
he is that saith to thee, Give me to drink, thou perhaps
wouldst have asked of him, and he would have given
thee living water" (*John* 4:10). He is opposing the new
Law of which He is the bearer to the old Law.

If it be so, one may ask whether Jacob's well is not
only an allusion to the Law of Israel but to the Essenian
community which represented itself as a new covenant.
We shall observe that the episode took place in Samaria, and Cullman has observed that, at the conclusion
of the account, verse 38 of the same chapter[17] appears
to be an allusion to a mission of the Hellenists in Samaria which we have already discussed Thus in this passage we would find a new point of contact between
John and the circles of the Hellenists, these converted
Zadokites who evangelized Samaria and Damascus and
who, above all, knew the *Damascus Document.*

Is the Epistle to the Hebrews Addressed to the Essenes?

Do we have any other evidence on the relations
between the books of the New Testament and the
Zadokite priests after 70 A. D.? I shall disregard the

[17]"I have sent you to reap that in which you did not labor: others
have labored and you have entered into their labors."

elements that one can find in the Catholic Epistles of Peter, James and Jude. But one text does merit our attention, this is the mysterious *Epistle to the Hebrews*. It presents features common to the thought of Paul, but it is not his and certainly came after him. And it is very difficult to determine its geographical locale: Father Spicq thinks it is Syria, Leonhard Goppelt, Rome, Father Braun, Asia-Minor; while most authors fix the background as Alexandria. But if the geographical location escapes us, the spiritual setting, on the other hand, can be determined.

We have already noted that the Zadokites seemed to make an extraordinary cult of angels: now the entire beginning of the Epistle is an affirmation of the superiority of the Word over the angels. Moreover the Zadokites are linked to a priestly group: the entire Epistle is centered on the question of the true priest, a central question with the Zadokites, expressed by their very name. Under the Maccabees they had been separated from the Jewish community because the high priests of the latter were Hasmoneans who did not descend from Aaron and Levi. Legitimists who remained loyal to the lineage of Zadok, the great Aaronid high priest of the time of Solomon, they were waiting for two Messiahs to come with the last days; one would be a high priest, the Messiah of Aaron, the other, subordinate to him, would be the Messiah of Judah.

For this reason it certainly must have been difficult for them to recognize Jesus as the Messiah. For if Jesus could pretend to be the Messiah, and the Son of David,

He was in no wise a descendant of Aaron and therefore could not be a sacerdotal Messiah. Now the purpose of the *Epistle to the Hebrews* is to show that Jesus is the Messianic High Priest and that it is not repugnant that the two functions be gathered in the same person. But it was still necessary to adduce an argument in support of this assertion. The author of the Epistle goes in search of one to Melchisedec, who was at once a priest and king. And he uses this as a basis for asserting that the true Messiah does not belong to the lineage of Aaron, but stems from an even higher levitical lineage: he is the high priest after the order of Melchisedec.

Clearly such a demonstration of the legitimacy of the priesthood, which appears very complicated to us, can be easily explained if its purpose was to convince a group for whom the question of the Aaronid priesthood was a central one. Hence it seems quite reasonable to view those to whom the Epistle was addressed as a group of Essenian priests.[18] The importance attached to the cult of the Temple would lead in the same direction; the same can also be said for a certain rigorism, not to speak of such expressions as "And to the church of the firstborn, who are written in the heavens" which designates the angels (12:23). Its very allegorical form, so distinctive of the *Epistle*, recalls what Philo says of the Essenes; and it would also correspond with a development of their exegesis which had been prophetic in the ancient *midrashim*, but which had gradually become more mystical. Does this permit us to

[18]BRAUN, *loc. cit.*, pp. 37-38.

determine the geographical locale of this text? It seems that this evolution of the Essenes was most marked in Egypt. There one finds the *Therapeutes,* a branch of the Essenian movement that perhaps goes back to the exile of the Teacher of Righteousness into Egypt. Perhaps it is a question here of the second exile, the one after 70 A. D. In any case Egypt would seem to be the locale indicated because of the contacts with Philo on the one hand, and the *Epistle of the Pseudo-Barnabas* on the other.

The Testaments of the XII Patriarchs — The Work of a Converted Essene

A study of the New Testament shows us that a great number of Zadokite priests were converted to Christianity: we have already noted the first movement of converts in Jerusalem, that of the Hellenists, who established the Church in Syria; later, after the fall of Jerusalem, we see St. John in Asia-Minor, and the author of the *Epistle to the Hebrews* in dialogues with dispersed Essenes. And it is highly probable that at that time many rallied to Christianity. We have certain proof of this in the form of certain writings whose sources up to now had been enigmatic but whose origins we have now discovered. These writings are the first ones in which we find Essenian influence to be so marked.

We have already spoken of the *Testaments of the*

XII Patriarchs. This work, preserved only in Greek, Armenian, and old Slavonic, reports the exhortations made by the twelve sons of Jacob to their children. Each one of them recommends a particular virtue, and each one likewise prophesies what will befall his descendants. This work gives rise to a singular question. In fact it offers so many similarities with the Qumran scrolls that it may be viewed as an Essenian document. This is evident in the characteristic expressions themselves: the name of Belial given to the demon, the "visitation of the Lord" which one finds in the *Manual of Discipline* (III, 18) and in *Luke* 19:44. The doctrine of the two spirits also holds an important place in this work, as well as the Gnosis of the mysteries. But there is something even more singular: in it one finds the conception of the waiting for a priestly Messiah, descending from the tribe of Levi—which is an absolute and specific feature of Qumran. One can also note in this work a certain predilection for the text in *Numbers* 24:17, so dear to the men of Qumran.

On the other hand the Christian character of the work is certain. Texts such as the following leave no doubt: "When God shall visit the world, He himself having come like a man among men, He will save Israel and all the nations, God wearing the face of man!" (*Asher* VII, 4). One reads further that "God assumed a body, and has eaten with men and saved man" (*Simeon* VI, 7). Of the Messiah it is said that "He will save all the nations and Israel" (*Simeon* VII, 2). The text in *Levi* IV, 1 is applied to the Passion of the Most

High which at one and the same time affirms the Crucifixion and the Divine Person of the Crucified. Christ
is called "Saviour of the World" (*Levi* X, 2), a specifically Christian expression found in *Luke* 2:11. Certain
expressions moreover are borrowed from the New Testament: "The Lamb of God who removes the sins of
the world will rise for us in order to save Israel and all
the nations" (*Joseph* XIX, 1). Many other doctrinal or
liturgical traits, which can leave no doubt of such borrowings, have been pointed out by de Jonge.

But we have another proof of the Christian origin of
this text and it is furnished to us by the Qumran excavations themselves. This proof is that no fragment of
this work has been found. Given the number of fragments of other documents that have been found there,
such an absence is decisive. Moreover, fragments of a
Testament of Levi have been found; but it is not similar
to the one that we know and it has no Christian character whatsoever. Thus it seems highly probable that with
the *Testaments of the XII Patriarchs* we are not dealing
with an Essenian work edited by a Christian, but an
actual Christian writing which was inspired by a literary genre in use at Qumran. Here, therefore, we have a
characteristic example of the literature of converted
Essenes.

The interest of the work lies in the fact that it revolves, in large measure, around the problem that we
have just posed in connection with the *Epistle to the
Hebrews*, the problem of the priestly Messiah. According to the Zadokites he had to be a descendant of Levi.

Now, just like the *Epistle,* the *Testaments* show a new priest in him: "After God shall have avenged himself of the wicked priests, the priest will disappear and the Lord will raise a new priest" (*Levi* XVIII, 1). This priest is described in the same terms as the Davidic Messiah which proves his identity with him: "His star will rise in the sky like a King, illuminating the light of knowledge . . . The heavens will open and from the sanctuary of glory sanctification will descend upon him along with the paternal voice. And the Spirit of holiness and intelligence will rest on him upon the waters. He will give the greatness of God to his sons and will have no successors. Under his priesthood sin will have an end. He will open up the gates of Paradise. And Belial will be bound by him" (*Levi* XVIII, 3-12).

One will note in this text the allusions to the Baptism of Christ, with the voice of the Father, the effusion of the Spirit and the waters of Jordan. Especially to be noted is the close resemblance with the *Apocalypse* of John which confirms our idea that the *Apocalypse* attests to links between John and the Syrian Hellenists, as Cullman has demonstrated. Finally, the resemblances between it and the *Epistle to the Hebrews* are striking. The idea that the Messianic High Priest will not have any successors can be found textually in the *Epistle to the Hebrews.* It will be observed that if the High Priest belongs to an order different from that of the Aaronid priesthood, the *Testaments,* however, make no allusion to Melchisedec. On the contrary this allusion to Melchisedec "chief of the priests of another race" is found in another work of this time, the *Second Book of Enoch* (XLI, 3-4) which must be linked to the same circles.

The Syrian Church and the Zadokites

It would seem that the *Testaments* originated in Syria. They therefore express the theology of the Christians who had come over from Essenism, had been converted in Jerusalem and had founded the Syrian Church. These were the Christians with whom John was in contact and among whom Paul was instructed. They constitute a particular group in the primitive Church: very influential, and distinct from that of James and of the Jerusalem community, and also distinct from the Pauline establishment in Asia-Minor and Rome. After the fall of Jerusalem in 70 A. D., Antioch was to become the center of Aramaic Christianity and give it its Essenian color. This Church of Antioch was to reach its high point under Ignatius, then lose its supremacy soon afterward when Hellenist Christianity began to grow and flourish. Nevertheless, it would preserve its special features up to our own time in Syriac Christianity, so impregnated with Judaism, so sacerdotal and so cultist.

The question then arises as to whether we have any other documents on this Antiochan Church whose members were partly recruited from Essenian circles. It so happens that the Church of Antioch is that on which we are the best informed as regards its ancient history. The first Christian ritual, the *Didache*, surely originated there, later around 120 A. D., we have the *Letters* of Ignatius of Antioch; and then a collection of liturgical *Psalms*, and the *Odes of Solomon* preserved in Syria. Now if we compare the facts concerning the organization of the ecclesiastic community contained in these works, they form a coherent image many of whose features recall Qumran It is quite probable that certain of these features go back to the primitive community of Jerusalem, and that is why we have talked about the latter. But the most typical features are distinctly Antiochan.

We have already observed that the catechism preparatory to baptism which the *Didache* presents us is structured on the *Treatise on the Two Ways*, an Essenian catechism about which we know through the *Manual of Discipline.* This doctrine of the ways marks, as we have also noted, other aspects of the preparation for baptism: the renunciation of Satan and the profession of faith in Christ are its culmination, which at Qumran had its equivalent in the break with the infidel Jews and their way, and the adhesion to the community and its way. From the *Clementine Homilies* we learn that this practice existed among the Judeo-Christians with whom the principal virtue that was recommended was simplicity — straightforwardness as opposed to duplicity, which is hesitation between the two ways.

Baptism was administered in running water. This is found in the pseudo-Clementine writings and seems to be Essenian. One must pray three times a day. And the practice of composing liturgical *Hymns* for the meetings of the community is attested to by Ignatius. We have admirable examples of these in the *Odes of Solomon*. These present great similarities to the *Hodayot* of Qumran, also composed for cultist gatherings. The expression "praise of the lips," so dear to Qumran and which is in the *Epistle to the Hebrews*, is found in the *Odes*. One will also note here the importance of the knowledge of the mysteries. The author of the *Odes* considers himself inspired, as does the author of the *Hodayot*. This reminds us of the place held by the prophets in the archaic communities. It will be noted that in the fourth century the Syriac deacon, Ephrem, also composed liturgical hymns.

On the other hand, in the *Letters* of Ignatius the community of Antioch appears to present a highly organized hierarchy. There is a bishop, then the presbyter, and then the deacons. Such a highly developed organization at so early a date has been a problem to scholars for a long time. It was way in advance of the Church organizations in Rome or in Asia Minor. Now we know that the hierarchic structure was a characteristic of Qumran, and this would be a powerful argument for asserting the Essenian origin of the Syrian community. Ignatius conceived his Church, as Campenhausen sees it, essentially as a community of praise structured along monastic lines[19] which strongly calls to mind the Qumran monastery and its liturgical cult.

[19]*Kirchliches Amt und geistliche Vollmacht in den ersten Jahrhunderten*, 1953, p. 113.

Another characteristic feature of the Syrian Church is its asceticism. We notice that wine is never mentioned in the *Odes of Solomon*. Milk and water provide the imagery But the essential thing is the attitude with regard to marriage. It is not condemned. And it is only condemned by extremists like Tatien. There is nothing special about the fact that virginity is praised. But it would clearly seem that virginity enjoyed a special status in the community. Vööbus has shown that at the moment of baptism one was asked to choose between marriage and celibacy, and those who chose celibacy were baptized first and occupied a higher rank. Other documents show something analogous. Thus Molland has shown that the organization of the Ebionites also presented two degrees, and that the higher degree was characterized by a higher level of asceticism which entailed virginity,[20] and which corresponds to that which we learn from the Qumran documents: in the Essenian community there was a higher degree of monks and a lower degree of married persons.

This is very interesting because it shows us the existence of a spiritual hierarchy alongside an institutional hierarchy. The monks were not marginal to the community as they are today, but represented its higher degree. And it is very probable that the priests and bishops were recruited among them, which made it possible for the two hierarchies to coincide to a great extent. It is because of this slant that the monasticism of Qumran can be considered as the source of Christian

[20]See *Studia Theologica*, IX (1955), pp. 37-39.

monasticism, not in that it was continued in a particular group, but insofar as it concerned the very structure of the ecclesiastic community.

Ebionism and Essenism

It remains to ask ourselves whether Syria was the only region where the Essenes, expelled from Palestine in 70 A. D., found refuge. We have said that the Gospel of John seems to address itself to those in Asia Minor. But we do not have any writings which attest with any certainty to their presence in that region. Moreover, we have said that the *Epistle to the Hebrews* was also aimed at Zadokite priests. We think that it is Alexandrian, but even here there is no text that would permit us to disclose with certainty the presence of any converted Essenes in Egypt. The only ancient texts that we have, the *Epistle to the Hebrews* and the Christian *Sibyllines*, are not decisive. On the contrary there are two regions where we certainly do find Christianized Essenes and these are at the two extreme poles of the Christian world of the time: in Trans-Jordan and in Rome.

In fact it is to Essenism that the heterodox group, the Ebionites, must be linked. This name comes from the Hebrew "ebion" which means "poor." It refers to a group of Jews who believed in Christ, but only as a great Jewish prophet and not as the risen Son of God. This group seems to have been organized in Trans-Jordan after 70 A. D., and it was still in existence in the fourth century and known to St. Jerome. It presents amazing similarities with Islam whose remote origins it could represent. We know the group well because of the accounts of Irenaeus, but above all because of two singular writings, the *Homilies* and the *Thanksgivings* of the pseudo-Clement.

Now this group presents such amazing similarities with the Zadokites that one author, Teicher, has been able to maintain that the Qumran manuscripts were their work.[21] If this seems impossible, it is at least certain, as Cullman in particular has shown, that we are dealing with a group that derived from Essenism.[22] They teach that God has established two beings, Christ and the Devil. Power over future time was given to the former, and power over the present to the latter. But, for them, Christ was not engendered of God the Father; He was created like one of the archangels, but He is greater than they. Each generation the Devil sends a false prophet and Christ a true prophet. Jesus is only one of these prophets, assisted by the Prince of Lights, the Christ. For them Paul was a prophet to whom Peter had been opposed . This hostility to Paul marks the close attachment of the Ebionites to the Jews.

They are, in fact, strict observers of the Jewish Law. They practice circumcision and observe the Sabbath. But they condemn the sacrifices of the Temple, thus

---

[21] "The Habakuk Scroll," *JJS*, V (1954), pp. 47-59.
[22] "Die neuentdeckten Qumrantexte und das Judenchristentum der Pseudo-Klementinen," *NTS für R. Bultmann*, pp. 35-51. See also H. J. Schoeps, "Handelt es sich Wirklich um ebionitische Dokumente," *ZRGG* (1953), pp. 242-255.

exaggerating the attitude of the Zadokites, who separated themselves from the Temple but who did not condemn the sacrifices and awaited their re-establishment in a purified Temple. Like the Essenes, they have daily ritual baths. But they also have a baptism of initiation, like the Christians. For their sacred meals they use unleavened bread and water, but they condemn the use of wine. This was not the rule at Qumran; but it is well in accordance with the rigorism of the Zadokites, some of whom at least proscribed wine.

All this permits us to trace the physiognomy of the group. They were surely Essenes. But, on the one hand, they have more radical tendencies: condemnation of the Temple, hostility to the priesthood, rejection of the books of the Prophets, and a rigorous asceticism. On the other hand, they have recognized in Jesus the supreme Incarnation of the True Prophet who manifests Himself to each generation; but they did not believe either in His Resurrection or in His Divinity. Thus they represent an intermediate group between Essenism and Christianity. In connection with them one can truly speak of a Christian Essenism, but one can also see how far they are from being a Christian community. And far from representing, as Schoeps thought, a survival of the primitive community of Jerusalem, this movement seems rather to be, as Cullman thinks, the result of an encounter with the Christianity of the Essenes who were exiled to Trans-Jordan after 70 A. D.[23]

[23]"Die neuendeckten Qumrantexte und das Judenchristentum der Pseudoklementinen," pp. 49-50.

An Essene Converted in Rome

The last Christian writing in which we can with certitude recognize the work of a converted Essene is located in quite different surroundings. It is entirely orthodox and reflects a Roman background. Hermas' *The Shepherd* is one of the most curious works of ancient Christian literature. It is a collection of visions, parables, and moral statements, which contain the revelations made by an angel, called *The Shepherd*. The oldest of these revelations go back to 90 A. D. In fact, the author was ordered to submit them to Pope Clement who reigned at that time and of whom, in addition, we have an *Epistle*. The last revelations date from around 140 A. D., during the pontificate of Pope Pius. According to the *Muratorian Canon*, the author, Hermas, was his brother. The Roman origin of the work is attested to by these allusions to the Bishop of Rome.

Scholars have always noted that this work presented marked Jewish features. But the discovery of the Dead Sea Scrolls has allowed a Canadian scholar, Audet, to go much further and to recognize beyond doubt the author as a converted Essene.[24] In fact the comparisons are decisive. The moral teachings are expounded in accordance with the doctrine of the two spirits. But, in addition, even the details are similar. The activity of the good spirit produces peace, benevolence, and joy; the evil spirit gives rise to disorder, bitterness, and

[24]"Affinités littéraires et doctrinales du Manuel de discipline." *RB*, LX (1953), pp. 41-82.

sadness. One point is particularly noteworthy. We have seen that for the Essenes the Prince of Light was identified with the Archangel Michael. We have also seen that the Christians had countered this with the tenet that the adversary of Satan was not an archangel, but the Word itself. Now Hermas presents a sort of a compromise between the two points of view. He identifies the Prince of Light with the Son of God, but he leaves him the name Michael (*Par; VIII, 1-3*).

This opens new perspectives on the origins of the Church of Rome. Rome had a considerable Jewish colony, as the Jewish catacombs discovered there have shown. Now these Jews represented widely different tendencies. Hence the groups of Christians converted from Judaism, who constituted the first community, also must have represented different tendencies. The first group was formed before the coming of the Apostles. Peter arrived among them, and then later Paul. Cullman is of the opinion that there were conflicts between the various tendencies and that Peter's martyrdom had been caused by a denunciation on the part of Christians of Judaizing tendencies.[25] Hence the presence of a converted Essene in Rome in the year 90 A. D., appears entirely normal.

Thus can be observed at one and the same time, the certainty and the complexity of the relations that exist between the Qumran documents and the origins of Christianity. Above all, what is striking is that the question poses itself at different stages which can be

[25]*Saint Pierre,* pp. 58-67.

summarized as follows: Three of these stages mainly involve the Zadokite community in the origins of Christianity: the first stage is pre-Christian, namely John the Baptist's membership in the Qumran community before beginning his distinctive vocation, the second is the conversion of Zadokite priests to Christianity in Jerusalem after the Pentecost, and the particular stamp which they gave to Syriac Christianity; the third stage is the entry into the Christian fold of many Essenes, following their dispersion in 70 A. D., and such conversions took place in all localities.

On the other hand Christ Himself is a stranger to the Essenian world. And He is particularly a stranger to it because of His background, which is Galilee, and because of His Davidic Messianism and, even more, because of His doctrine and His works which are in complete contrast with Essenian doctrine and the life of the Teacher of Righteousness. The only points of contact concern practical customs, calendars, and structure of the community, in which Christ and the Apostles seem to have been inspired by what they saw in the most fervent Jewish communities of their time. This is true of the authors of the New Testament, and of John and Paul in particular. They borrowed forms of thought from Essenism, just like Origen and Clement were to borrow them from Philo, but the content of their doctrine is as different as the faith of Nicaea is from the doctrines of Timaeus.

The fact remains that, by acquainting us with the immediate settings against and within which Chris-

tianity was born, the Qumran discoveries have resolved
a considerable number of problems for which exegesis
was not able to find satisfactory answers: the early
background of John the Baptist, the exact date of
Easter, the origin of the hierarchy, the vocabulary of
St. John, and the origin of Gnosticism. It is probable
that the utilization of all the documents, and the comparisons to which they will give rise, will add consider-
ably to the number of enigmas that will be solved.
Hence one can say that this discovery is one of the most
sensational that has ever been made. This momentous
discovery provides us with the setting in which Christianity was born and shows us much that has been
preserved within these historic times; and certainly, it
helps us to see wherein the unique and distinctive
character of Christianity lies.